The Best-Dressed

Knitted Bear

The Best-Dressed
Knitted Bear

Dozens of Patterns for Teddy Bears, Bear Costumes, and Accessories

Emma King

POTTER
CRAFT

New York

This book is dedicated to my Nan

Published in the United States by Potter Craft, an
imprint of the Crown Publishing Group, a division of
Random House, Inc., New York.

www.crownpublishing.com
www.pottercraft.com

POTTER CRAFT and colophon is a registered
trademark of Random House, Inc.

Originally published in the United Kingdom by Collins
& Brown, an imprint of Anova Books Company Ltd,
London.

Library of Congress Cataloging-in-Publication Data
is available upon request.

ISBN 978-0-307-45382-2

Printed in China by 1010 Printing International Ltd

10 9 8 7 6 5 4 3 2 1

First American Edition

The author and publisher would like to thank the
Craft Yarn Council of America for providing the yarn
weight standards and accompanying icons used in
this book. For more information, please visit
www.YarnStandards.com.

Contents

Introduction 7

Simple Small Bear 8

Princess Bear 10

Wizard Bear 13

Tooth Fairy Bear 16

Simple Medium-Sized Bear 20

Pirate Bear 23

Ballerina Bear 29

Springtime Bear 31

Intermediate Medium-Sized Bear 34

Hula Bear 37

Robin Hood Bear 39

Cheerleader Bear 44

Intermediate Large Bear 48

Fisherman Bear 51

Graduation Bear 56

Aladdin Bear 59

Complex Medium-Sized Bear 62

Safari Bear 67

Newborn Baby Bear 71

Cowboy Bear 75

Complex Large Bear 80

First Birthday Bear 83

Swimmer Bear 89

Golfer Bear 90

Yarn and Gauge 94

Abbreviations 94

Resources 95

Acknowledgments 96

Introduction

Whether it's tropical fun with Hula Bear, swashbuckling adventures with Pirate Bear or a magical time with Wizard Bear, *The Best-Dressed Knitted Bear* has a bear for every occasion.

I have had great fun creating this collection of knitted bears and their many outfits. Mixing traditional with contemporary styles I have designed a collection of six different bears ranging in size and complexity from a simple small-sized bear through to a large, more complicated bear.

The simple bear has minimum shaping and the body is knit in one piece, as is the head. The intermediate bear has more shaping, the body is knit in two pieces, and the head has sides and a gusset. The complex bear again has more shaping and also has the added interest of contrasting yarns and colors used to create the snout and the paws. There is also a jointed option for the complex bear. Each of these basic bears has a delightful wardrobe of outfits to choose from.

You can choose to knit the bears in the colors that I have selected, or you might want to personalize them by changing the color or the yarn used. Information about alternative colors and yarns has been provided, so you can choose whether to knit your bear in a plain yarn or a tweed, or perhaps give your bear a touch of luxury by knitting it in silk or cashmere!

Why not knit a bear as a special gift? Golfer Bear would make an ideal present for any dad who loves to hit the links, and Safari Bear is perfect for the adventurers among us. These adorable bears are also a great way to mark an occasion—Newborn Baby Bear for a new arrival, Graduation Bear to celebrate the end of college, or First Birthday Bear for that important milestone. Or, why not simply choose a bear to knit as a treat for yourself?

I have used color, texture, sequins, and many more techniques to bring the bears to life, and I hope you have as much fun knitting them as I had creating them.

emma king

Simple Small Bear

This little bear is easy to knit—you'll soon have a cute little friend to dress up as a princess, wizard, or tooth fairy!

FINISHED SIZE
Height: 8" (20cm)
Diameter (around body): 6¼" (16cm)

MATERIALS
Option A (Beige)
- 126 yds (115m) sport weight yarn **2** fine
  The bear on page 11 uses 1 ball Rowan
  Cotton Glace, 100% cotton, 1 oz (50g),
  137 yds (115m), 730 Oyster

Option B (Cream)
- 126 yds (115m) sport weight yarn **2** fine
  The bear on page 14 uses 1 ball Rowan
  Cotton Glace, 725 Ecru
- Size 3 (3.25mm) needles (or size needed to
  obtain gauge)
- 175 yds (160m) sport weight yarn **2** fine
  for facial features. The bear on page 11
  uses a small amount of Rowan Calmer,
  75% cotton, 25% acrylic, 1 oz (50g),
  175 yds (160m), 481 Coffee Bean
- Tapestry needle
- 1 oz (50g) toy stuffing

GAUGE
23 stitches and 32 rows to 4" (10cm) using
size 3 (3.25mm) needles and sport weight yarn,
measured over stockinette stitch.

BODY
Cast on 11 stitches.
Row 1: Purl.
Row 2: K1, (m1, k1) to end—21 stitches.
Row 3: Purl.
Row 4: K2, m1, (k1, m1) to last 2 stitches,
k2—39 stitches.
Row 5: Purl.
Row 6: Knit.

Repeat rows 5 and 6 11 more times.
Row 29: Purl.
Row 30: K2tog, (k2, k2tog) to last 3 stitches,
k3—30 stitches.
Row 32: Purl.
Row 33: K2tog to end—15 stitches.
Row 34: Purl.
Row 35: K1 (k2tog) to end—8 stitches.
Do not bind off. Thread yarn through the
remaining stitches and pull together to secure.

HEAD
Cast on 9 stitches.
Row 1: Purl.
Row 2: K1, (m1, k1) to end—17 stitches.
Row 3: Purl.
Row 4: K1, (m1, k1) to end—33 stitches.
Row 5: Purl.
Row 6: Knit.
Row 7: Purl.
Row 8: K2, (m1, k4) to last 3 stitches, m1,
k3—41 stitches.
Row 9: Purl.
Row 10: Knit.
Repeat rows 9 and 10 5 more times.
Row 21: Purl.
Row 22: K1, (k2tog) to end—21 stitches.
Row 23: Purl.
Row 24: Knit.
Row 25: Purl.
Row 26: K1, (k2tog) to end—11 stitches.
Row 27: Purl.
Do not bind off. Thread yarn through the
remaining stitches and pull together to secure.

LEGS (MAKE 2)
Cast on 8 stitches.
Row 1: Purl.

Row 2: K1, (m1, k1) to end—15 stitches.
Row 3: Purl.
Row 4: K1, m1, (k3, m1) to last 2 stitches,
k2—20 stitches.
Row 5: Purl.
Row 6: K6, (k2tog) 4 times, k6—16 stitches.
Row 7: Purl.
Row 8: Knit.
Repeat rows 7 and 8 9 more times.
Next row: Purl.
Next row: K2tog to end—8 stitches.
Next row: Purl.
Do not bind off. Thread yarn through the
remaining stitches and pull together to secure.

ARMS (MAKE 2)
Cast on 7 stitches.
Row 1: Purl.
Row 2: K1, (m1, k1) to end—13 stitches.
Row 3: Purl.
Row 4: Knit.
Repeat rows 3 and 4 10 more times.
Next row: Purl.
Next row: K1, (k2tog) to end—7 stitches.
Do not bind off. Thread yarn through the
remaining stitches and pull together to secure.

EARS (MAKE 2)
Cast on 5 stitches.
Row 1: K1, p3, k1.
Row 2: K1, m1, k3, m1, k1—7 stitches.
Row 3: K1, p5, k1.
Row 4: Knit.
Bind off, leaving a tail long enough to shape
the ear and to attach it to the head.

FINISHING

HEAD, BODY, ARMS, LEGS

Each part of the bear has been knitted all in 1 piece, so will have only 1 seam. On the head and body, the seam will run from top to bottom down the center back of the piece. With each piece, start joining the seams at the top and work ⅔ of the way down the piece, then use the opening to stuff the piece until it is firm (the body should be approximately 6¼" (16cm) in diameter). Sew up the remaining ⅓ of the seam. Fasten securely.

SHAPING THE NOSE

To create the snout, a running stitch is made, then pulled slightly to create a three-dimensional shape. Using the photo on page 11 as a guide, and working toward the lower section of the face, sew a length of yarn in a circular shape. When you are happy with the shape, fasten the yarn securely. If you don't get the right shape the first time, leave the "wrong" circle of yarn threaded, and use this as a guide to help you get a better shape. Pull the "wrong" one out afterward.

FACIAL FEATURES

Using the brown yarn (Rowan Calmer shade 481), sew the bear's facial features as follows:

Nose and mouth

The nose is an upside-down triangle. Using the photograph as a guide, mark where you want the nose to be.

Stitch the nose as follows: Insert the needle into the snout and take it horizontally under 2 stitches and then out. Now insert needle just below where it originally went in and, again, take it horizontally under 2 stitches, then out

just below the previous stitch. Continue in this way, ensuring you shorten each consecutive stitch so the nose tapers to a point.

Stitch the mouth as follows: With the same yarn, starting at the tip of the snout, sew a long single stitch roughly ⅜" (1cm) down and insert the needle into the head, then bring it out ¼" (0.75cm) to the left and slightly lower. Create a diagonal single stitch by inserting the needle back in through the base of the ⅜" (1cm) vertical stitch. Then bring the needle back out ¼" (0.75cm) to the right and slightly lower (opposite to last time) and create a second diagonal stitch by inserting the needle back in through the base of the ⅜" (1cm) vertical stitch. Take the needle down through the head and out through the underside. Fasten securely.

Eyes

Measure approximately ⅝" (1.5cm) up from the top of the nose and place a marker. Each eye will be positioned roughly ¼" (0.75cm) to either side of this marker. Stitch the eyes as follows: Leaving a long tail for securing, insert the needle into the right-hand side of where the eye will be, then, taking it horizontally to the left and under 1 stitch, bring the needle back out. Take the yarn back through once more in the same way. Then insert the needle into the original hole and, this time, take it down through the head and out through the underside. Return to the long thread you left at the beginning. Thread this onto your needle and insert it into the hole to the left of the eye. Take it down through the center of the head and out through the underside. Pulling gently on these 2 yarns will set the eyes further into the bear's head, giving your bear's face character. When you have sewn both eyes, pull

gently on these yarns to create a face you are happy with. Then secure the yarns firmly to keep the features you have created.

EARS

Mark the position of the ears as follows: Measure ⅝" (1.5cm) to either side of center seam—this is where the ear will start. There will be a 1¼" (3cm) gap between the ears. Using the long thread that you left when binding off, give the ear some shape by weaving the thread around the outer edge of the ear and then use the same thread to attach the ear to the head.

ASSEMBLING YOUR BEAR

Sew the head securely to the top center of the body. Stitch the arms to the body at the shoulder approximately ¾" (2cm) down from the head. Sew the legs to the sides of the body, approximately ⅜" (1cm) up from the base of the torso.

Princess Bear

Little girls (and bigger girls too!) are certain to fall in love with Princess Bear. Her elegant dress and crown are finished with gorgeous beads and her soft mohair bodice is truly regal.

SKILL LEVEL
Intermediate

MATERIALS
For the dress and crown
- 126 yds (115m) sport weight yarn (2) fine (A). The bear's outfit opposite uses 1 ball Rowan Cotton Glace, 100% cotton, 1 oz (50g), 137 yds (115m), 828 Heather
- 229 yds (210m) sport weight yarn (2) fine used double throughout (B). The bear's outfit opposite uses 1 ball Rowan Kidsilk Haze, 70% super kid mohair, 30% silk, 7/8 oz (25g), 229 yds (210m), 579 Splendour

For the crown
- 191 yds (175m) fingering weight yarn (1) superfine (C). The bear's outfit opposite uses Rowan Shimmer, 60% cuprol, 40% polyester, 7/8 oz (25g), 191 yds (175m), 92 Silver
- Size 3 (3.25mm) needles (or size needed to obtain gauge)
- 500 approximately 3mm beads, such as Rowan 01014 in mauve
- Tapestry needle

GAUGE
23 stitches and 32 rows to 4" (10cm) using size 3 (3.25mm) needles and sport weight yarn, measured over stockinette stitch.

ABBREVIATIONS
PB Place Bead: Bring the yarn forward, slip bead to front of the work, slip 1 stitch purlwise, take the yarn to the back of work. The bead will now be sitting in front of the slipped stitch.

P2B Place 2 Beads: Bring the yarn forward, slip 2 beads to the front of the work, slip 1 stitch purlwise, take the yarn to the back of the work. The beads will now be sitting in front of the slipped stitch.

DRESS
Skirt (make 2 for front and back)
Using size 3 (3.25mm) needles and A, cast on 19 stitches.
Row 1(WS): Purl.
Row 2: K1, (PB, k1) to end.
Row 3: Purl.
Row 4: K2, (PB, k1) to last 3 stitches, PB, k21.
Row 5: Purl.
Row 6: K1, (PB, k1) to end.
Row 7: Purl.
Row 8: K1, PB, (m1, k1, m1, PB) to last stitch, k1—35 stitches.
Row 9: Purl.
Row 10: K1, PB, (k3, PB) to last stitch, k1.
Row 11: Purl.
Row 12: K1, PB, (k1, m1, k1, m1, k1, PB) to last stitch, k1—51 stitches.
Row 13: Purl.
Row 14: K1, PB, (k5, PB) to last stitch, k1.
Row 15: Purl.
Repeat rows 14 and 15 16 more times, ending with a wrong-side row.
Bind off.

Bodice (make 2 for front and back)
With right side facing and using size 3 (3.25mm) needles and B, pick up and knit 18 stitches along the cast-on edge of one of the skirt sections, and work as follows:

Row 1: Purl.
Row 2: K3, m1, (k4, m1) to last 3 stitches, k3—22 stitches.
Row 3: Purl.
Row 4: Knit.
Row 5: Purl.
Repeat rows 4 and 5 3 more times, ending with a wrong-side row.
Row 12: K6, turn and work on these 6 stitches only as follows:
Row 13: Purl.
Row 14: Knit to last 3 stitches, k2tog, k1—5 stitches.
Row 15: Purl.
Row 16: Knit to last 3 stitches, k2tog, k1—4 stitches.
Row 17: Purl.
Do not bind off. Leave the shoulder stitches on a holder.
Rejoin yarn to remaining stitches, bind off center 10 stitches, and knit to end. Work on these 6 stitches only as follows:
Row 13: Purl.
Row 14: K1, k2togtbl, knit to end—5 stitches.
Row 15: Purl.
Row 16: K1, k2togtbl, knit to end—4 stitches.
Row 17: Purl.
Do not bind off. Leave the shoulder stitches on a holder.

Neckband
Join the right shoulder using the three-needle bind off technique as described on page 26. With right side facing, using size 3 (3.25mm) needles and A, pick up and knit 6 stitches

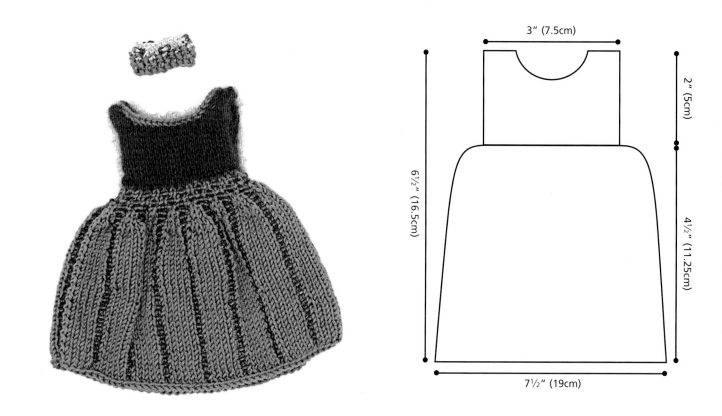

down the left front of the neck, 10 stitches across the center front, 6 stitches up the right front of the neck, 6 stitches down the right back of the neck, 10 stitches across the center back, and 6 stitches up the left back of the neck—44 stitches.
Bind off purlwise.

CROWN

Using size 3 (3.25mm) needles and A, cast on 19 stitches.
Row 1: K1, (p1, k1) to end.
Repeat this row once more.
Change to yarn C.
Repeat row 1 twice more.

Row 5: K1, P2B, (k3, P2B) to last stitch, k1.
Bind off.

FINISHING
Dress

Join the left shoulder using the three-needle bind off technique as described on page 26. Join the side seams of the skirt section of the dress, leaving the side seams of the bodice section open.

Crown

Whip stitch together the side seams of the crown.

Wizard Bear

Conjure up some fun with this magical little bear. Complete with a hat, cape, and wand, Wizard Bear will soon have everyone under his spell.

SKILL LEVEL
Intermediate

MATERIALS
For the cape and hat
- 191 yds (175m) fingering weight yarn (1) superfine. The bear's outfit on page 14 uses 1 ball Rowan 4ply Soft, 100% Merino wool, 1oz (50g), 191 yds (175m), 383 Black
- Approximately 250 6mm sequins, such as Gutterman 1000 Black
- 10 silver star sequins in assorted sizes from 5mm to 14mm
- Sizes 2 and 3 (3mm and 3.25mm) needles (or size needed to obtain gauge)
- Tapestry needle

GAUGE
28 stitches and 36 rows to 4" (10cm) using size 3 (3.25mm) needles and Rowan 4 ply Soft measured over stockinette stitch.

ABBREVIATION
PS Place Sequin: Bring the yarn forward, slip a sequin to the front of the work, slip 1 stitch purlwise, take the yarn to the back of the work. The sequin will now be sitting in front of the slipped stitch.

CAPE
Using size 3 (3.25mm) needles, cast on 47 stitches.
Row 1: K1, (PS, k1) to end.
Row 2: K1, purl to last stitch, k1.
Row 3: K2, (PS, k1) to last 3 stitches, PS, k2.
Row 4: K1, purl to last stitch, k1.
Row 5: K1, (PS, k1) to end.

Row 6: K1, purl to last st, k1.
Row 7: K2, (PS, k1) to last 3 stitches, PS, k2.
Row 8: K1, purl to last stitch, k1.
Row 9: K1, (PS, k1) to end.
Row 10: K1, purl to last stitch, k1.
Row 11: K2, (PS, k1) twice, k2togtbl, knit to last 8 stitches, k2tog, (k1, PS) twice, k2.
Row 12: K1, p5, p2tog, purl to last 8 stitches, p2togtbl, p5, k1.
Row 13: K1, PS, (k1, PS) twice, k2togtbl, knit to last 8 stitches, k2tog, PS (k1, PS) twice, k1.
Row 14: K1, p5, p2tog, purl to last 8 stitches, p2togtbl, p5, k1.
Row 15: K2, (PS, k1) twice, k2togtbl, knit to last 8 stitches, k2tog, (k1, PS) twice, k2.
Row 16: K1, p5, p2tog, purl to last 8 stitches, p2togtbl, p5, k1—35 stitches.
Row 17: (K1, PS) three times, knit to last 6 stitches, (PS, k1) to end.
Row 18: K1, purl to last stitch, k1.
Row 19: K2, PS, k1, PS, knit to last 5 stitches, PS, k1, PS, k2.
Row 20: K1, purl to last stitch, k1.
Repeat rows 19 and 20 until work measures 5⅛" (13cm) from cast-on edge, ending with a wrong-side row.
Next row: K2, (PS, k1) twice, k2togtbl, knit to last 8 stitches, k2tog, (k1, PS) twice, k2.
Next row: K1, p5, p2tog, purl to last 8 stitches, p2togtbl, p5, k1.
Next row: K1, PS (k1, PS) twice, k2togtbl, knit to last 8 stitches, k2tog, PS (k1, PS) twice, k1.
Next row: K1, p5, p2tog, p to last 8 stitches, p2togtbl, p5, k1.
Next row: K2, (PS, k1) to last 3 stitches, PS, k2.
Bind off.

HAT
Cone sections (make 3)
Using size 2 (3mm) needles, cast on 11 stitches.
Row 1: Knit.
Row 2: Purl.
Row 3: Knit.
Row 4: Purl.
Row 5: K1, k2togtbl, knit to last 3 stitches, k2tog, k1—9 stitches.
Row 6: Purl.
Row 7: Knit.
Row 8: Purl.
Row 9: Knit.
Row 10: Purl.
Row 11: K1, k2togtbl, knit to last 3 stitches, k2tog, k1—7 stitches.
Repeat rows 6 through 11 once more— 5 stitches.
Repeat rows 6 through 10 once more.
Next row: K1, sl2, k1, p2sso, k1—3 stitches.
Next row: Purl.
Next row: Sl2, k1, p2sso.
Fasten off.
Join all 3 sections along side seams, leaving the last side seam open, and then work brim as follows:
Brim
Pick up and knit 28 stitches along the cast-on edge of the 3 joined cone sections.
Row 1 (WS): Knit.
Row 2: K4, (m1, k4) to end—34 stitches.
Row 3: Knit.
Row 4: K1, m1, k10, m1, k12, m1, k10, m1, k1—38 stitches.
Row 5: Knit.

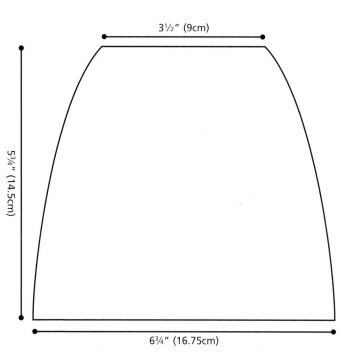

The measurements shown: 3½" (9cm) across the top, 5¾" (14.5cm) down the side, and 6¾" (16.75cm) across the bottom.

Row 6: K1, m1, k12, m1, k12, m1, k12, m1, k1—42 stitches.
Row 7: Knit.
Row 8: K1, m1, k14, m1, k12, m1, k14, m1, k1—46 stitches.
Row 9: Knit.
Bind off.

FINISHING

CAPE

Make the tie at the front of cape as follows: Cut a length of yarn approximately 6" (15cm) long. Tie a knot at one end and thread on 4 or 5 of the different-sized star sequins. Stitch the other end of the yarn to the left front opening of the cape at the bound-off edge. Repeat for the right front opening of the cape.

HAT

Sew together the final seam of the hat by stitching from the edge of the brim all the way to the top of the cone.

Tooth Fairy Bear

This gorgeous bear just loves to help the Tooth Fairy. Put her under your pillow and her little drawstring pouch will be full of money by morning!

SKILL LEVEL
Intermediate

MATERIALS
For the dress, wings and pouch
- 126 yds (115m) sport weight yarn 🔢 fine (A). The bear's outfit opposite uses 1 ball Rowan Cotton Glace, 100% cotton, 1¾ oz (50g), 137 yds (115m), 831 Dawn Grey
- 229 yds (210m) sport weight yarn 🔢 fine, used double throughout (B). The bear's outfit opposite uses 1 ball Rowan Kidsilk Haze, 70% super kid mohair, 30% silk, ⅞ oz (25g), 229 yds (210m), 580 Grace
- Sizes 2 and 3 (3mm and 3.25mm) needles (or size needed to obtain gauge)
- Approximately 30 3mm clear beads, such as Rowan 01008
- Approximately 5" (12cm) white elastic
- Tapestry needle

GAUGE
23 stitches and 32 rows to 4" (10cm) using size 3 (3.25mm) needles and sport weight yarn measured over stockinette stitch.

ABBREVIATION
PB Place Bead: Bring the yarn forward, slip bead to the front of the work, slip 1 stitch purlwise, take the yarn to the back of the work. The bead will now be sitting in front of the slipped stitch.

DRESS (MAKE 2 FOR FRONT AND BACK)
First frill section
Using size 3 (3.25mm) needles and B, cast on 81 stitches.
Change to yarn A.
Row 1: K1, *k2, lift the first of these 2 stitches over the second, repeat from * to end.
Row 2: (P2tog) to last stitch, p1—21 stitches.
Row 3: Knit.
Row 4: Purl.
Repeat rows 3 and 4 twice more.
Break off yarn. Leave the stitches on a holder.

Second frill section
Using size 3 (3.25mm) needles and B, cast on 81 stitches.
Change to yarn A.
Row 1: K1, *k2, lift the first of these 2 stitches over the second, repeat from * to end.
Row 2: (P2tog) to last stitch, p1—21 stitches.
Join the second frill section to the first frill section as follows:
With right sides facing, knit together the first stitch on the needle with the first stitch on the holder. Continue in this way until the whole row has been completed.
Next row: Purl.
Next row: Knit.
Next row: Purl.
Repeat the last 2 rows once more.
Break off yarn and leave these stitches on a holder.

Third frill section
Using size 3 (3.25mm) needles and B, cast on 81 stitches.
Change to yarn A.
Row 1: K1, *k2, lift the first of these 2 stitches over the second, repeat from * to end—41 stitches.
Row 2: (P2tog) to last stitch, p1—21 stitches.
Join the third frill section to the second frill section as follows:
With right sides facing, knit together the first stitch on the needle with the first stitch on the holder. Continue in this way until the whole row has been completed.
Row 4: Purl.
Row 5: Knit.
Row 6: Purl.
Repeat the last 2 rows 7 more times, ending with a wrong-side row.
Row 21: Knit.
Row 22: K1, p19, k1.
Row 23: K7, turn and work on these 7 stitches only as follows:
Row 24: K1, p5, k1.
Row 25: K1, k2togtbl, k1, k2tog, k1—5 stitches.
Row 26: K1, p1, k1.
Row 27: K1, sl2, k1, p2sso, k1—3 stitches.
Row 28: K1, p1, k1.
Row 29: Knit.
Row 30: K1, p1, k1.
Repeat the last 2 rows once more, ending with a wrong-side row.

Do not bind off. Break off yarn and leave the shoulder stitches on a holder.

With right side facing, rejoin yarn to remaining stitches and work as follows:

Row 23: Bind off center 7 stitches, knit to end.

Row 24: K1, p5, k1.

Row 25: K1, k2togtbl, k1, k2tog, k1—5 stitches.

Row 26: K1, p3, k1.

Row 27: K1, sl2, k1, p2sso, k1—3 stitches.

Row 28: K1, p1, k1.

Row 29: Knit

Row 30: K1, p1, k1.

Repeat the last 2 rows once more, ending with a wrong-side row.

Do not bind off. Leave the shoulder stitches on a holder.

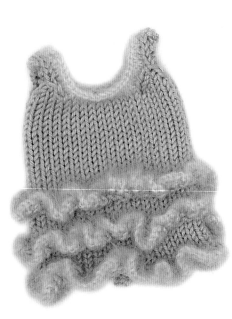

NECKBAND

Join the right shoulder using the three-needle bind off technique as described on page 26. With right side facing, and using size 2 (3mm) needles and B, pick up and knit 10 stitches down the left front of the neck, 7 stitches across the center front, 10 stitches up the right front of the neck, 10 stitches down the right back of the neck, 7 stitches across the center back, and 10 stitches up the left back of the neck—54 stitches.

Next row: Purl.

Bind off.

WINGS (MAKE 2)

Using size 2 (3mm) needles and A, cast on 5 stitches.

Row 1: Knit.

Row 2: K1, p3, k1.

Repeat rows 1 and 2 once more.

Row 5: K1, m1, knit to last stitch, m1, k1—7 stitches.

Row 6: K1, p5, k1.

Row 7: K1, m1, PB, knit to last 2 stitches, PB, m1, k1—9 stitches.

Row 8: K1, purl to last stitch, k1.

Repeat rows 7 and 8 until there are 25 stitches, ending with a wrong-side row.

Row 25: K1, (PB, k1) to end.

Row 26: Knit. (This creates the ridge for the turn-over at the edge of the wing.)

Row 27: Knit.

Row 28: K1, purl to last stitch, k1.

Row 29: K1, k2togtbl, knit to last 3 stitches, k2tog, k1—23 stitches.

Repeat rows 28 and 29 until 5 stitches remain.

Row 48: K1, p3, k1.

Row 49: Knit.

Row 50: K1, p3, k1.

Bind off.

DRAWSTRING POUCH

Side (make 2)

Using size 3 (3.25mm) needles and B, cast on 25 stitches.

Row 1: K1, *k2, lift the first of these 2 stitches over the second, repeat from * to end—13 stitches.

Row 2: (P2tog) to last stitch, p1—7 stitches. Change to yarn A.

Row 3: Knit.

Row 4: Purl.

Row 5: K1, yo, k2tog, k1, yo, k2tog, k1.

Row 6: Purl.

Row 7: K1, m1, knit to last stitch, m1, k1—9 stitches.

Row 8: Purl.

Row 9: Knit.

Row 10: Purl.

Repeat rows 9 and 10 twice more, ending with a wrong-side row.

Do not bind off. Leave the stitches on a holder.

FINISHING
DRESS

Join the left shoulder using the three-needle bind off technique as described on page 26.

Join the front and back sections of the dress as follows: leaving a 1⅝" (4cm) opening at the top of each seam for the armhole, join side seams.

WINGS

Each wing has a front and a back section which are separated by a garter stitch ridge. Fold along the garter stitch ridge so that your wing becomes double layered, and then whip stitch the side seams of the 2 layers together as neatly as possible. Repeat for the other wing. With the beaded side as the right side, stitch the narrowest edges of the 2 wings together.

Finally, sew a loop of elastic to each of the wings on either side of the center seam. These loops can then be hooked over the bear's arms.

DRAWSTRING POUCH

Join the 2 bottom seams of the pouch using the three-needle bind-off technique as described on page 26.
Sew the side seams.
Cut 2 strands of yarn, approximately 16" (40.5cm) in length. Make twisted cord as described below:

Technique for making twisted cord:

Take the strands of yarn and secure at each end with knots. Ask someone to help you and give them one end of the yarn while you hold the other. With the yarn stretched out, twist each end in opposite directions until it shows signs of twisting back on itself. Bring the 2 ends of the cord together and hold tightly, allowing the 2 halves to twist together. Smooth out any bumps by running your fingers up and down the cord.

You will now have a twisted cord measuring approximately 6½" (16.5cm). If you would like a longer cord, start off with longer lengths.

Make a knot at each end of the cord, then thread the cord through eyelet holes near the frill, and tie the ends together.

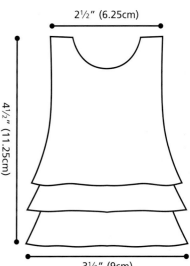

Simple Medium-Sized Bear

Dress this bear as a pirate, a ballerina, or in a pretty springtime outfit—the choice is yours. Easy to knit and adorable in any color, this bear is perfect as a gift or to keep for yourself.

FINISHED SIZE
Height: 10¾" (27cm)
Diameter (around body): 7¾" (20cm)

MATERIALS
Option A (Beige)
- 93 yds (85m) worsted weight yarn (4) medium. The bear on page 28 uses 1 ball Rowan Handknit Cotton, 100% cotton, 1 oz (50g), 93 yds (85m), 205 Linen

Option B (Dark beige)
- 93 yds (85m) worsted weight yarn (4) medium. The bear on page 22 uses 1 ball Rowan Handknit Cotton, 205 Tope
- Size 5 (3.75mm) needles (or size needed to obtain gauge)
- 175 yds (160m) sport weight yarn (2) fine for facial features. The bear on page 28 uses a small amount of Rowan Calmer, 75% cotton, 25% acrylic, 1 oz (50g), 175 yds (160m), 481 Coffee Bean
- Tapestry needle
- 1¾ oz (50g) toy stuffing

GAUGE
22 stitches and 29 rows to 4" (10cm) using size 5 (3.75mm) needles and worsted weight yarn, measured over stockinette stitch.

BODY
Cast on 11 stitches.
Row 1: Purl.
Row 2: K1, (m1, k1) to end—21 stitches.
Row 3: Purl.
Row 4: K2, m1, (k1, m1) to last 2 stitches, k2—39 stitches.
Row 5: Purl.
Row 6: Knit.
Repeat rows 5 and 6 11 more times.
Row 29: Purl.
Row 30: K2, k2tog, (k2, k2tog) to last 3 stitches, k3—30 stitches.
Row 31: Purl.
Row 32: (K2tog) to end—15 stitches.
Row 33: Purl.
Row 34: K1 (k2tog) to end—8 stitches.
Do not bind off. Thread yarn through the remaining stitches and pull together to secure.

HEAD
Cast on 9 stitches.
Row 1: Purl.
Row 2: K1, (m1, k1) to end—17 stitches.
Row 3: Purl.
Row 4: K1, (m1, k1) to end—33 stitches.
Row 5: Purl.
Row 6: Knit.
Row 7: Purl.
Row 8: K2, (m1, k4) to last 3 stitches, m1, k3—41 stitches.
Row 9: Purl.
Row 10: Knit.
Repeat rows 9 and 10 5 more times.
Row 21: Purl.
Row 22: K1, (k2tog) to end—21 stitches.
Row 23: Purl.
Row 24: Knit.
Row 25: Purl.
Row 26: K1, (k2tog) to end—11 stitches.
Row 27: Purl.
Do not bind off. Thread yarn through the remaining stitches and pull together to secure.

LEGS (MAKE 2)
Cast on 8 stitches.
Row 1: Purl.
Row 2: K1, (m1, k1) to end—15 stitches.
Row 3: Purl.
Row 4: K1, m1, (k3, m1) to last 2 stitches, k2—20 stitches.
Row 5: Purl.
Row 6: K6, (k2tog) 4 times, k6—16 stitches.
Row 7: Purl.
Row 8: Knit.
Repeat rows 7 and 8 9 more times.
Next row: Purl.
Next row: (K2tog) to end—8 stitches.
Next row: Purl.
Do not bind off. Thread yarn through the remaining stitches and pull together to secure.

ARMS (MAKE 2)
Cast on 7 stitches.
Row 1: Purl.
Row 2: K1, (m1, k1) to end—13 stitches.
Row 3: Purl.
Row 4: Knit.
Repeat rows 3 and 4 10 more times.
Next row: Purl.
Next row: K1, (k2tog) to end—7 stitches.
Do not bind off. Thread yarn through the remaining stitches and pull together to secure.

EARS (MAKE 2)
Cast on 5 stitches.
Row 1: K1, p3, k1.
Row 2: K1, m1, k3, m1, k1—7 stitches.
Row 3: K1, p5, k1.
Row 4: Knit.

Bind off, leaving a long enough thread to shape the ear and attach it to the head.

FINISHING
HEAD, BODY, ARMS, LEGS
Each part of the bear has been knitted all in 1 piece, so will have only 1 seam. On the head and body, the seam will run from top to bottom down the center back of the piece. With each piece, start joining the seams at the top and work ⅔ of the way down the piece, then use the opening to stuff the piece until it is firm (the body should be approximately 7¾" (20cm) in diameter). Sew up the remaining ⅓ of the seam. Fasten securely.

SHAPING THE NOSE
To create the snout, a running stitch is made, then pulled slightly to create a three-dimensional shape. Using the photograph on page 22 as a guide, and working toward the lower section of the face, sew a length of yarn in a circular shape. When you are happy with the shape, fasten the yarn securely. If you don't get the right shape the first time, leave the "wrong" circle of yarn threaded, and use this as a guide to help you get a better shape. Pull the "wrong" one out afterward.

FACIAL FEATURES
Using the brown yarn (Rowan Calmer shade 481), sew the bear's facial features as follows:

Nose and mouth
The nose is an upside-down triangle. Using the photograph as a guide, mark where you want the nose to be.

Stitch the nose as follows: Insert the needle into the snout and take it horizontally under 3 stitches and then out. Now insert needle just

below where it originally went in and, again, take it horizontally under 3 stitches, then out just below the previous stitch. Continue in this way, ensuring you shorten each consecutive stitch so the nose tapers to a point.

Stitch the mouth as follows: With the same yarn, starting at the tip of the snout, sew a long single stitch roughly ½" (1.25cm) down and insert the needle into the head, then bring it out ¼" (0.75cm) to the left and slightly lower. Create a diagonal single stitch by inserting the needle back in through the base of the ½" (1.25cm) vertical stitch. Then bring the needle back out ¼" (0.75cm) to the right and slightly lower (opposite to last time) and create a second diagonal stitch by inserting the needle back in through the base of the ½" (1.25cm) vertical stitch. Take the needle down through the head and out through the underside. Fasten securely.

Eyes
Measure approximately ¾" (2cm) up from the top of the nose and place a marker. Each eye will be positioned roughly ⅝" (1.5cm) to either side of this marker. Stitch the eyes as follows: Leaving a long tail for securing, insert the needle into the right-hand side of where the eye will be, then, taking it horizontally to the left and under 1 stitch, bring the needle back out. Take the yarn back through once more in the same way. Then insert the needle into the original hole and, this time, take it down through the head and out through the underside. Return to the long thread you left at the beginning. Thread this onto your needle and insert it into the hole to the left of the eye. Take it down through the center of the head and out through the underside. Pulling gently on these 2 yarns will set the eyes further into the bear's head, giving your bear's face

character. When you have sewn both eyes, pull gently on these yarns to create a face you are happy with. Then secure the yarns firmly to keep the features you have created.

EARS
Mark the position of the ears as follows: Measure ⅝" (1.75cm) either side of center seam—this is where the ear will start. There will be a 1⅜" (3.5cm) gap between the ears. Using the long thread that you left when binding off, give the ear some shape by weaving the thread around the outer edge of the ear and then use the same thread to attach the ear to the head.

ASSEMBLING YOUR BEAR
Sew the head securely to the top center of the body. Stitch the arms to the body at the shoulder approximately 1¼" (3cm) down from the head. Sew the legs to the sides of body, approximately ⅝" (1.5cm) from the base of the torso.

Pirate Bear

Ready to sail the seven seas, Pirate Bear is sure to be a hit with adventurers young and old. His ruffled shirt, pirate hat, and sword give him a real swashbuckling look.

SKILL LEVEL
Intermediate

MATERIALS
For the pants
- 123 yds (113m) DK weight yarn **3** light (A). The bear's outfit opposite uses 1 ball Rowan Scottish Tweed DK, 100% wool, 1 oz (50g), 142 yds (130m), 023 Midnight

For the shirt
- 126 yds (115m) sport weight yarn **2** fine (B). The bear's outfit opposite uses 1 ball Rowan Cotton Glace, 100% cotton, 1 oz (50g), 137 yds (115m), 726 Bleached

For the belt, hat, and sword handle
- 126 yds (115m) sport weight yarn **2** fine (C). The bear's outfit opposite uses 1 ball Rowan Cotton Glace, 727 Black

For the sash
- 175 yds (160m) sport weight yarn **2** fine (D). The bear's outfit opposite uses 1 ball Rowan Calmer, 75% cotton, 25% acrylic, 1 oz (50g), 175 yds (160m), 492 Garnet

For the sword
- 191 yds (175m) fingering weight yarn **1** superfine (E). The bear's outfit opposite uses a small amount of Rowan Shimmer, 60% cuprol, 40% polyester, ⅞ oz (25g), 191 yds (175m), 92 Silver
- ¾" (2cm) buckle
- Sizes 3 and 6 (3.25mm and 4mm) needles (or size needed to obtain gauge)
- Size 2 (3mm) double-pointed needles (or size needed to obtain gauge)
- Tapestry needle

GAUGE
PANTS
22 stitches and 30 rows to 4" (10cm) using size 6 (4mm) needles and DK weight yarn, measured over stockinette stitch.

SHIRT
23 stitches and 32 rows to 4" (10cm) using size 3 (3.25mm) needles and sport weight yarn, measured over stockinette stitch.

VEST
25 stitches and 34 rows to 4" (10cm) using size 6 (4mm) needles and sport weight yarn, measured over stockinette stitch.

PANTS

Front

Leg (make 2)

Using size 6 (4mm) needles and A, cast on 7 stitches.

Row 1: Purl.

Row 2: K1, (m1, k1) to end—13 stitches.

Row 3: Purl.

Row 4: K1, k2, m1, (k3, m1) to end—17 stitches.

Row 5: Purl.

Row 6: Knit.

Row 7: Purl.

Repeat rows 6 and 7 7 more times, ending with a wrong-side row.

Do not bind off. Leave the stitches on a holder.

Join the two legs of the front as follows:

With right sides facing, knit across 16 stitches of the left leg, knit the last stitch of the left leg together with the first stitch of the right leg, knit to end—33 stitches.

Next row: Purl.

Next row: K2, k2tog, (k1, k2tog) to last 2 stitches, k2—23 stitches.

Next row: Purl.

Next row: Knit.

Next row: Purl.
Repeat the last 2 rows 4 more times.
Bind off.

Back

Work as for the Front.

SHIRT

Back

Using size 3 (3.25mm) needles and B, cast on 29 stitches.

Row 1: Knit.

Row 2: Purl.

Repeat rows 1 and 2 13 more times, ending with a wrong-side row.

Next row: K8, bind off center 13 stitches, k8.

Do not bind off. Leave the 2 sets of shoulder stitches on a holder.

Front

Using size 3 (3.25mm) needles and B, cast on 29 stitches.

Row 1: Knit.

Row 2: Purl.

Repeat rows 1 and 2 9 more times, ending with a wrong-side row.

Row 21: K12, turn and work on these stitches only as follows:

Row 22: K1, purl to end.

Row 23: Knit to last 3 stitches, k2tog, k1—11 stitches.

Row 24: K1, purl to end.

Row 25: Knit to last 3 stitches, k2tog, k1—10 stitches.

Repeat rows 24 and 25 twice more—8 stitches.

Row 30: K1, purl to end.

Do not bind off. Leave the shoulder stitches on a holder.

With right side facing, rejoin the yarn to the remaining stitches and work as follows:

Next row: Bind off center 5 stitches, knit to end—12 stitches.

Next row: Purl to last stitch, k1.

Next row: K1, k2togtbl, knit to end—11 stitches.

Next row: Purl to last stitch, k1.

Next row: K1, k2togtbl, knit to end—10 stitches.

Repeat the last 2 rows twice more—8 stitches.

Next row: Purl to last stitch, k1.

Do not bind off. Leave the shoulder stitches on a holder.

SLEEVES (MAKE 2)

Using size 3 (3.25mm) needles and B, cast on 73 stitches

Row 1: K1, *k2, lift first of these 2 stitches over second, repeat from * to end—37 stitches.

Row 2: (P2tog) to last stitch, p1—19 stitches.

Row 3: Knit.

Row 4: Purl.

Row 5: K1, (m1, k1) to end—37 stitches.

Row 6: Purl.

Row 7: Knit.

Repeat rows 6 and 7 4 more times, ending with a right-side row.

Next row: P1, (p2tog) to end—19 stitches.

Bind off.

FRILL COLLAR

Using size 3 (3.25mm) needles and B, cast on 93 stitches.

Row 1: K1, *k2, lift first of these 2 stitches over second, repeat from * to end—47 stitches.

Row 2: (P2tog) to last stitch, p1—24 stitches.
Bind off.

VEST

Left front

Using size 6 (4mm) needles and D, cast on 7 stitches.

Row 1: Knit.

Row 2: K1, p5, k1.

Repeat rows 1 and 2 twice more, ending with a wrong-side row.

Row 7: K1, m1, knit to end—8 stitches.

Row 8: K1, purl to last stitch, k1.

Row 9: Knit.

Row 10: K1, purl to last stitch, k1.

Row 11: K1, m1, knit to end—9 stitches.

Repeat rows 8 through 11 twice more—11 stitches.

***Row 20:** K1, p9, k1.

Row 21: Knit.

Row 22: K1, p9, k1.

Repeat rows 21 and 22 4 more times, ending with a wrong-side row.

Row 31: K1, k2togtbl, knit to last 3 stitches, k2tog, k1—9 stitches.

Row 32: K1, p9, k1.

Row 33: K1, k2togtbl, knit to last 3 stitches, k2tog, k1—7 stitches.

Repeat rows 32 and 33 once more—5 stitches.

Row 36: K1, p3, k1.

Row 37: K1, sl2, k1, p2sso, k1—3 stitches.

Row 38: K1, p1, k1.

Row 39: K3tog.
Fasten off.

Right front

Using size 6 (4mm) needles and D, cast on 7 stitches.

Row 1: Knit.

Row 2: K1, p5, k1.

Repeat rows 1 and 2 twice more, ending with a wrong-side row.

Row 7: Knit to last stitch, m1, k1—8 stitches.

Row 8: K1, purl to last stitch, k1.

Row 9: Knit.

Row 10: K1, purl to last stitch, k1.

Row 11: K to last stitch, m1, k1—9 stitches.

Repeat rows 8 through 11 twice more—11 stitches.

Work as for left front from * to end.

Back

With right side facing and using size 6 (4mm) needles and D, pick up and knit 7 stitches along the cast-on edge of the left front, turn, and cast on 11 stitches, turn, and pick up and knit 7 stitches along the cast-on edge of the right front—25 stitches.

Row 1: K1, purl to last stitch, k1.

Row 2: Knit.

Repeat rows 1 and 2 13 more times, ending with a right-side row.

Row 29: K1, p23, k1.

Row 30: K1, k2togtbl, knit to last 3 stitches, k2tog, k1—23 stitches.

Row 31: K1, p2tog, purl to last 3 stitches, p2togtbl, k1—21 stitches.

Repeat rows 30 and 31 until 5 stitches remain.

Row 40: K1, sl2, k1, p2sso, k1—3 stitches.

Next row: P3tog.
Fasten off.

BELT

Using size 3 (3.25mm) needles and C, cast on 5 stitches.

Row 1: Knit.

Row 2: K1, p1, k1.

Repeat rows 1 and 2 until belt measures 11⅝" (29cm) from cast-on edge.
Bind off.

HAT

Peak

Using size 3 (3.25mm) needles and C, cast on 5 stitches.

Row 1: K1, (m1, k1) to end—9 stitches.

Row 2: Purl.

Row 3: K1, (m1, k1) to end—17 stitches.

Repeat rows 2 and 3 1 more time—33 stitches.

Row 6: Purl.

Row 7: Knit.

Row 8: Purl.

Repeat rows 7 and 8 once more, ending with a wrong-side row.
Bind off.

SASH

Using size 3 (3.25mm) needles and D, cast on 4 stitches.

Row 1: Knit.

Row 2: K1, p2, k1.

Repeat rows 1 and 2 until sash measures 10¼" (26cm) from cast-on edge.

Bind off.

SWORD

Blade

Using the technique described below, make the sword blade out of an I-cord as follows:

Using size 2 (3mm) double-pointed needles and E, cast on 5 stitches.

Row 1: Knit.

Repeat this row until cord is 1⅝" (4cm) long.

Next row: K2tog, k1, k2tog.

Next row: Knit.

Next row: K3tog.

Fasten off.

Technique for making I-cord: Once you have cast on your stitches, you must knit 1 row. You would now usually turn your needles, but to make the cord, do not turn. Instead, slide the stitches to the other end of the double-pointed needle ready to be knitted again. The yarn will now be at the left edge of the knitting and so to knit, you must pull it tightly across the back of your work and then knit 1 row. You continue in this way, never turning, and always sliding the work to the other end of the double-pointed needle. The right side of the work will always be facing you.

SWORD HANDLE

Using size 3 (3.25mm) needles and C, cast on 14 stitches.

Row 1: Knit.

Row 2: (P2tog) to end—7 stitches.

Row 3: Knit.

Row 4: Purl.

Bind off.

FINISHING

PANTS

Join the front and back of the pants as follows: Sew the outer side seams—start at the top (the bound-off edge) and work down to the bottom (the cast-on edge). Now, join the inner leg seams starting at the cast-on edge of the right leg, working up to the top, and then working down the corresponding seam of the left leg.

SHIRT

Slip the right front shoulder stitches and the right back shoulder stitches onto needles. Join the right shoulder seam using the three-needle bind-off technique given below, then repeat for the left shoulder seam.

Three needle bind-off: This technique allows you to join 2 pieces of knitting by binding them off together instead of sewing them together. The method is worked by placing the 2 pieces of knitting (each piece on a needle) together in the left hand with right-sides facing each other. With a third needle, bind off the 2 rows of stitches together. Insert the right needle through the stitch on the front needle and through the stitch on the back needle and work them together. Repeat and bind off in the usual way.

Collar

Stitch the bound-off edge of the frill collar to the front neck edge starting at one shoulder, working down the front neck, across the center neck, and then up the other side of the neck.

Sleeves

Fold the sleeve in half lengthwise and mark the center of the bound-off edge with a stitch marker. Line this marker up with the shoulder seam and tack the sleeve in place, then sew the sleeve to the body. Attach both sleeves in the same way.

Join both side and sleeve seams.

VEST

Sew side seams, leaving 2" (5cm) open near the shoulder edges for armholes.

HAT

Join the peak to the sash as follows: Measure approximately 1⅝" (4cm) from the cast-on edge of the sash, along the side seam. Place a marker. Starting at the marker, stitch the bottom edge of the peak (the side seams and the original 5 cast on stitches) to the side of the sash. There should then be approximately 5⅛" (13cm) of sash remaining. Using the photograph as a guide, coil the sash around and sew the bound-off edge of the sash to the wrong-side side of the sash at the point where the marker is.

BELT

Thread the buckle onto one end of the belt.

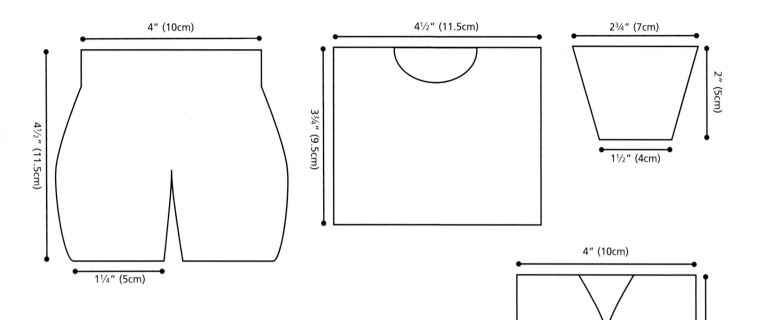

SWORD

Sew the 2 side edges of the handle together, creating a cupped shape. Stitch the cast-on edge of the blade into the center of the cup and secure. Thread a loop of yarn through the handle so that the sword can be carried by the bear if desired.

SKILL LEVEL
Intermediate

MATERIALS
For the skirt, cardigan and ballet slippers

- 175 yds (160m) sport weight yarn (2) fine (A). The oufit for the bear on this page uses 1 ball Rowan Calmer, 75% cotton, 25% acrylic, 1 oz (50g), 124 yds (113m), 488 Sugar
- 229 yds (210m) sport weight yarn (2) fine (B). The outfit for the bear on this page uses 1 ball Rowan Kidsilk Haze, 70% super kid mohair, 30% silk, ⅞ oz (25g), 229 yds (210m), 634 Cream
- Size 6 (4mm) needles (or size needed to obtain gauge)
- Approximately 170 6mm iridescent sequins, such as Gutterman 1050
- Approximately 27½″ (70cm) of ⅛″ (3mm) -wide cream ribbon
- Tapestry needle

GAUGE
25 stitches and 34 rows to 4″ (10cm) using size 6 (4mm) needles and sport weight yarn, measured over stockinette stitch.

ABBREVIATION
ML Place sequin on a loop. Knit into the next stitch and, before slipping the stitch off the left needle, slide a sequin up to the needle and bring the yarn to the front of the work between the needle points. Wrap the yarn around your left thumb and take it back between the needle

Ballerina Bear

Pretty in pink, Ballerina Bear is ready and waiting to dance for you. Her gorgeous ballet shoes are laced with ribbons and her tutu is covered with beautiful sequins to catch the light as she twirls.

points. Now, knit into the stitch again and then slip the stitch off the needle. You will now have two stitches on the right-hand needle. Bind one off by lifting one stitch over the other.

SKIRT
Using size 6 (4mm) needles and A, cast on 51 stitches.
Row 1: K1, (p1, k1) to end.
Row 2: Repeat row 1.
Row 3: Knit.
Row 4: Purl.
Row 5: K3, (m1, k5) to last 3 stitches, m1, k3—61 stitches.
Row 6: Purl.
Row 7: K1, (ML, k1) to end.
Row 8: Purl.
Row 9: K2, (ML, k1) to last 3 stitches, ML, k2.
Row 10: Purl.
Row 11: K1, (ML, k1) to end.
Row 12: P1, m1, p3 (m1, p3) to end—81 stitches.
Row 13: K1, (ML, k1) to end.
Row 14: Purl.
Row 15: K2, (ML, k1) to last 3 stitches, ML, k2.
Row 16: Purl.
Row 17: (K1, m1) to last stitch, k1—161 stitches.
Bind off.

CARDIGAN
Back
Using size 6 (4mm) needles and B doubled, cast on 25 stitches.
Change to yarn A.

Row 1: K1, (p1, k1) to end.
Row 2: Repeat row 1.
Row 3: Knit.
Row 4: Purl.
Repeat rows 3 and 4 10 more times, ending with a wrong-side row.
Row 25: K4, bind off center 17 stitches, knit to end.
Do not bind off. Leave the 2 sets of shoulder stitches on a holder.

Right front
Using size 6 (4mm) needles and B doubled, cast on 25 stitches.
Change to yarn A.
Row 1: K1, (p1, k1) to end.
Row 2: Repeat row 1.
Row 3: Knit.
Row 4: Purl to last stitch, k1.
Row 5: K1, k2togtbl, knit to end—24 stitches.
Row 6: Purl to last 3 stitches, p2togtbl, k1—23 stitches.
Repeat rows 5 and 6 until 4 stitches remain.
Do not bind off. Leave the shoulder stitches on a holder.

Left front
Using size 6 (4mm) needles and B doubled, cast on 25 stitches.
Change to yarn A.
Row 1: K1, (p1, k1) to end.
Row 2: Repeat row 1.
Row 3: Knit.
Row 4: K1, purl to end.
Row 5: Knit to last 3 stitches, k2tog, k1.

Row 6: K1, p2tog, purl to end.
Repeat rows 5 and 6 until 4 stitches remain.
Do not bind off. Leave the shoulder stitches on a holder.

SLEEVES
Using size 6 (4mm) needles and B doubled, cast on 19 stitches.
Change to yarn A.
Row 1: K1, (p1, k1) to end.
Row 2: Repeat row 1.
Row 3: Knit.
Row 4: Purl.
Repeat rows 3 and 4 6 more times, ending with a wrong-side row.
Bind off.

BALLET SLIPPERS
Using size 6 (4mm) needles and A, cast on 4 stitches.
Row 1: Purl.
Row 2: K1, (m1, k1) to end—7 stitches.
Repeat rows 1 and 2 once more—13 stitches.
Row 5: Purl.
Row 6: K1, (m1, k2) to end—19 stitches.
Row 7: Purl.
Row 8: (K4, m1) twice, k3, (m1, k4), m1, knit to end—23 stitches.
Row 9: Purl.
Row 10: Knit.
Row 11: Purl.
Row 12: K8, turn and work on these 8 stitches only as follows:
Row 13: Purl.
Row 14: Knit.

Repeat rows 13 and 14 3 more times.
Row 21: Purl.
Bind off.
Rejoin yarn to remaining stitches, bind off center 7 stitches, and knit to end. Working on these 8 stitches only, continue as follows:
Next row: Purl.
Next row: Knit.
Repeat these 2 rows 3 more times.
Next row: Purl.
Bind off.

FINISHING

SKIRT

The skirt has been knitted all in 1 piece. Sew together the side seam.

CARDIGAN

Join both shoulder seams using the three-needle bind-off technique as described on page 26.

Sleeves

Fold sleeve in half lengthwise and mark the center of the bound-off edge with a marker. Line this marker up with the shoulder seam and tack the sleeve in place. Now sew the sleeve to the body. Attach both sleeves in the same way.
Join both side and sleeve seams.

BALLET SLIPPERS

Fold slipper in half and sew the 2 side edges together—this creates a seam at the center back. Using a tapestry needle and the photograph as a guide, lace 13¾" (35cm) of ribbon up the front of each slipper.

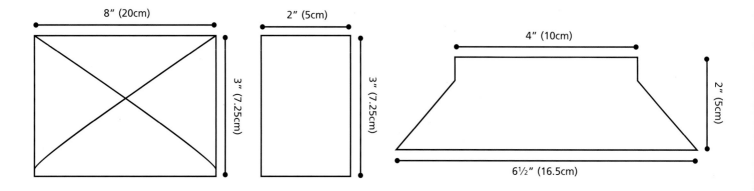

8" (20cm)

3" (7.25cm)

2" (5cm)

3" (7.25cm)

4" (10cm)

2" (5cm)

6½" (16.5cm)

Springtime Bear

Springtime Bear loves collecting wild flowers in her favorite yellow dress.

SKILL LEVEL
Simple

MATERIALS

For the dress
- 175 yds (160m) sport weight yarn **2** fine (A). The bear's outfit on page 32 uses 1 ball Rowan Calmer, 75% cotton, 25% acrylic, 1oz (50g), 175 yds (160m), 494 Freesia

For the basket
- 126 yds (115m) sport weight yarn **2** fine (B). The bear's outfit on page 32 uses 1 ball Rowan Cotton Glace, 100% cotton, 1 oz (50g), 137 yds (115m), 730 Oyster

For the flowers
- 126 yds (150m) sport weight yarn **2** fine in 4 shades—2 appropriate for flowers and 2 shades of green for leaves. The bear's outfit on page 32 uses small amounts Rowan Cotton Glace in the following shades: 724 Bubbles, 832 Persimmon, 814 Shoot, and 812 Ivy
- 229 yds (210m) sport weight yarn **2** fine in 2 shades appropriate for flowers. The bear's outfit on page 32 uses small amounts Rowan Kidsilk Haze, 70% super kid mohair, 30% silk, 7/8 oz (25g), 229 yds (210m) in the following shades: 606 Candy Girl and 579 Splendour
- 93 yds (85m) aran weight yarn **4** medium in a shade appropriate for flowers. The bear's outfit on page 32 uses small amount Rowan Handknit Cotton, 100% cotton, 1 oz (50g), 92 yds (85m), 305 Lupin
- Sizes 3 and 6 (3.25mm and 4mm) needles (or size needed to obtain gauge)
- Small amount of toy stuffing
- Tapestry needle

GAUGE
25 stitches and 34 rows to 4" (10cm) using sport weight yarn and size 6 (4mm) needles, measured over stockinette stitch.

DRESS (MAKE 2 FOR FRONT AND BACK)
Using size 6 (4mm) needles and A, cast on 43 stitches.
Row 1: K1, (p1, k1) to end.
Repeat row 1 3 more times, ending with a wrong-side row.
Row 5: Knit.
Row 6: Purl.
Row 7: K1, k2togtbl, knit to last 3 stitches, k2tog, k1—41 stitches.
Row 8: Purl.
Row 9: Knit.
Row 10: Purl.
Row 11: K1, k2togtbl, knit to last 3 stitches, k2tog, k1—39 stitches.
Repeat rows 8 through 11 until 25 stitches remain.
Row 40: Purl.
Row 41: K9, turn and work on these 9 stitches only as follows:
Row 42: Purl.
Row 43: Knit to last 3 stitches, k2tog, k1—8 stitches.
Repeat rows 42 and 43 until 5 stitches remain.
Row 50: Purl.
Row 51: Knit.
Row 52: Purl.
Do not bind off. Leave the shoulder stitches on a holder.
With right side facing, rejoin yarn to remaining stitches and work as follows:
Next row: Bind off center 7 stitches, knit to end.
Next row: Purl.
Next row: K1, k2togtbl, knit to end.
Repeat the last two rows until 5 stitches remain.
Next row: Purl.
Next row: Knit.
Next row: Purl.
Do not bind off. Leave the shoulder stitches on a holder.

NECKBAND
Join the right shoulder using the three-needle bind-off technique as described on page 26. With right side facing and size 6 (4mm) needles, pick up and knit 12 stitches down the left front of the neck, 8 stitches across the center front, 12 stitches up the right front of the neck, 12 stitches down the right back of the neck, 8 stitches across the center back, and 12 stitches up the left back of the neck—64 stitches.
Row 1: (K1, p1) to end.
Bind off in seed stitch.

Row 12: K1, k2togtbl, knit to last 3 stitches, k2tog, k1—9 stitches.
Repeat rows 11 and 12 twice more—5 stitches.
Row 17: Purl.
Row 18: K1, sl2, k1, p2sso, k1.
Row 19: Purl.
Bind off.

Handle
Using size 3 (3.25mm) needles and B, cast on 3 stitches.
Row 1: Knit.
Row 2: K1, p1, k1.
Repeat rows 1 and 2 until handle measures 5½" (14cm) from cast-on edge, ending with a wrong-side row.
Bind off.

FLOWERS
Flower with hot pink trim
Using size 3 (3.25mm) needles and Kidsilk Haze shade 606, cast on 49 stitches.
Change to Cotton Glace shade 724.
Row 1: K1, *k2, lift the first of these 2 stitches over the second, repeat from * to end—25 stitches.
Row 2: (P2tog) to last stitch, p1—13 stitches.
Do not bind off. Thread the yarn through the remaining stitches and pull, gathering it around into a flower shape, and then secure.

Pink flower
Using size 3 (3.25mm) needles and Cotton Glace shade 724, cast on 33 stitches.
Row 1: K1, *k2, lift the first of these 2 stitches over the second, repeat from * to end—17 stitches.
Row 2: (P2tog) to last stitch, p1—9 stitches.
Do not bind off. Thread the yarn through the remaining stitches and pull, gathering it around into a flower shape, and then secure.

SLEEVES (MAKE 2)
Using size 6 (4mm) needles and A, cast on 19 stitches.
Row 1: K1, (p1, k1) to end.
Repeat this row once more, ending with a wrong-side row.
Row 3: Knit.
Row 4: Purl.
Repeat rows 3 and 4 4 more times, ending with a wrong-side row.
Bind off.

BASKET
Side (make 2)
Using size 3 (3.25mm) needles and B, cast on 7 stitches.
Row 1: Purl.
Row 2: Increase in first stitch by knitting in the front and back of the stitch, yfwd, sl1, ybk, (k1, yfwd, sl1, ybk) to last stitch, increase in last stitch—9 stitches.
Repeat rows 1 and 2 until there are 19 stitches.
Row 13: K1, (yfwd, sl1, ybk, k1) to end.
Row 14: Purl.

Row 15: K2, yfwd, sl1, ybk, (k1, yfwd, sl1, ybk) to last 2 stitches, k2.
Row 16: Purl.
Row 17: Purl. (This creates the ridge for a turn-over hem at the top of the basket.)
Row 18: Purl.
Row 19: Knit.
Row 20: Purl.
Bind off.

Lid
Using size 3 (3.25mm) needles and B, cast on 3 stitches.
Row 1: Purl.
Row 2: K1, (m1, k1) to end—5 stitches.
Row 3: Purl.
Row 4: K1, m1, k3, m1, k1—7 stitches.
Row 5: Purl.
Row 6: K1, m1, k5, m1, k1—9 stitches.
Row 7: Purl.
Row 8: K1, m1, k7, m1, k1—11 stitches.
Row 9: Purl.
Row 10: Knit.
Row 11: Purl.

Flower with dark purple trim (make 2)
Using size 3 (3.25mm) needles and Kidsilk Haze
shade 579, cast on 29 stitches.
Change to Handknit Cotton shade 305.
Row 1: K1, *k2, lift the first of these 2 stitches
over the second, repeat from * to end—
15 stitches.
Row 2: (P2tog) to last stitch, p1—8 stitches.
Do not bind off. Thread the yarn through the
remaining stitches and pull, gathering it around
into a flower shape, and then secure.

Lilac flower
Using size 3 (3.25mm) needles and Handknit
Cotton shade 305, cast on 25 stitches.
Row 1: K1, *k2, lift the first of these 2 stitches
over the second, repeat from * to end—
13 stitches.
Row 2: (P2tog) to last stitch, p1—7 stitches.
Do not bind off. Thread the yarn through the
remaining stitches and pull, gathering it around
into a flower shape, and then secure.

Orange flower
Using size 3 (3.25mm) needles and Cotton
Glace shade 832, cast on 29 stitches.
Row 1: K1, *k2, lift the first of these 2 stitches
over the second, repeat from * to end—
15 stitches.
Row 2: (P2tog) to last stitch, p1—8 stitches.
Do not bind off. Thread the yarn through the
remaining stitches and pull, gathering it around
into a flower shape, and then secure.

LEAVES
Make 5 leaves—2 in Cotton Glace shade 814,
and 3 in Cotton Glace shade 812, as follows:
Using size 3 (3.25mm) needles, cast on 3 stitches.
Row 1: K1, p1, k1.
Row 2: K1, m1, k1, m1, k1—5 stitches.
Row 3: K1, p3, k1.
Row 4: K2, m1, k1, m1, k2—7 stitches.

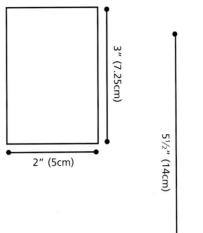

Row 5: K1, p5, k1.
Row 6: K2, sl2, k1, psso 2, k2—5
stitches.
Row 7: K1, p3, k1.
Row 8: K1, sl2, k1, p2sso, k1—3
stitches.
Row 9: Sl2, k1, p2sso—1 stitch.
Fasten off.

FINISHING
DRESS
Join the left shoulder seam using the three-
needle bind-off technique as described on
page 26.

Sleeves
Fold sleeve in half lengthwise and mark the
center of the bound-off edge with a marker.
Line this marker up with the shoulder seam
and tack the sleeve in place. Then sew the
sleeve to the body. Attach both sleeves in the
same way.
Join side and sleeve seams. Using the
photograph as a guide, sew one of the flowers
with dark purple trim to the front left neck of
the dress.

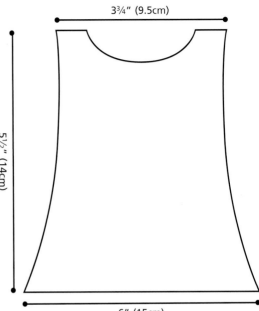

FLOWER BASKET
Basket
Fold hem inside the top of the basket and slip
stitch into place. Do this for both sides. Join the
2 sides by sewing down 1 side, across the
bottom and up the other side. Next, fill the
basket with toy stuffing up to the slip-stitched
hem. Insert the lid into the top of the basket
(covering and sealing in the toy stuffing) and
whip stitch to the hem. Now, using the
photograph as a guide, sew the remaining
flowers and leaves to the lid of the basket,
making a nice arrangement.

Intermediate Medium-Sized Bear

Once you've mastered the simple bears, why not move on to this new friend? Doing the hula in Hawaii, cheering for your favorite sports team, or shooting arrows as Robin Hood, this bear is ready for adventure.

FINISHED SIZE
Height: 10¾" (27cm)
Diameter (around body): 7¾" (20cm)

MATERIALS
Option A (Beige)
- 246 yds (226m) DK weight yarn ③ light. The bear on page 38 uses 2 balls Rowan Wool Cotton, 50% wool, 50% cotton, 1 oz (50g), 123 yds (113m), 929 Dream

Option B (Cream)
- 246 yds (226m) DK weight yarn ③ light. The bear on page 40 uses 2 balls Rowan Wool Cotton, 900 Antique
- 175 yds (160m) sport weight yarn ② fine. for facial features. The bear on page 38 uses a small amount Rowan Calmer, 75% cotton, 25% acrylic, 1 oz (50g), 175 yds (160m), 481 Coffee Bean
- Size 3 (3.25mm) needles (or size needed to obtain gauge)
- Tapestry needle
- Long sewing needle
- 1¾ oz (50g) toy stuffing

GAUGE
26 stitches and 32 rows to 4" (10cm) using size 3 (3.25mm) needles and DK weight yarn, measured over stockinette stitch.

BODY
Sides (make 2)
Cast on 9 stitches.
Row 1 (RS): Knit.
Row 2: Purl.
Row 3: K4, m1, k1, m1, k4—11 stitches.

Row 4: Purl.
Keeping shaping as set (increasing on either side of the center stitch), repeat rows 3 and 4 until there are 21 stitches, ending with a wrong-side row.
Row 14: Knit.
Row 15: Purl.
Row 16: K10, m1, k1, m1, k10—23 stitches.
Row 17: Purl.
Row 18: Knit.
Row 19: Purl.
Repeat rows 18 and 19 11 more times.
Row 42: K9, k2togtbl, k1, k2tog, knit to end—21 stitches.
Row 43: Purl.
Row 44: K8, k2togtbl, k1, k2tog, knit to end—19 stitches.
Row 45: P7, p2tog, p1, p2togtbl, purl to end—17 stitches.
Row 46: K6, k2togtbl, k1, k2tog, knit to end—15 stitches.
Row 47: P5, p2tog, p1, p2togtbl, purl to end—13 stitches.
Row 48: K4, k2togtbl, k1, k2tog, knit to end—11 stitches.
Row 49: P3, p2tog, p1, p2togtbl, purl to end—9 stitches.
Row 50: (K2tog) 4 times, k1—5 stitches.
Do not bind off. Thread yarn through the remaining stitches and pull together to secure.

HEAD
Left side
Using size 3 (3.25mm) needles, cast on 13 stitches.
Row 1: Knit.

Row 2: Purl.
Repeat rows 1 and 2 once more.
Row 5: K1, m1, knit to last stitch, m1, k1—15 stitches.
Row 6: Purl.
Repeat rows 5 and 6 once more.
Row 9: Knit to last stitch, m1, k1—18 stitches.
Row 10: P1, m1, purl to end—19 stitches.
Repeat rows 9 and 10 once more.
Row 13: Knit to last stitch, m1, k1—22 stitches.
Row 14: Purl.
Row 15: Knit.
Repeat rows 14 and 15 twice more.
Row 20: Bind off 5 stitches, purl to end—17 stitches.
Row 21: Knit to last 3 stitches, k2tog, k1—16 stitches.
Row 22: Bind off 4 stitches, purl to end—12 stitches.
Row 23: Knit.
Row 24: Purl.
Row 25: K1, k2tog, knit to last 3 stitches, k2tog, k1—10 stitches.
Row 26: P1, p2tog, purl to last 3 stitches, p2tog, p1—8 stitches.
Bind off.

Right side
Using size 3 (3.25mm) needles, cast on 13 stitches.
Row 1: Knit.
Row 2: Purl.
Row 3: Knit.
Row 4: P1, m1, purl to last stitch, m1, p1—15 stitches.

Row 5: Knit.
Repeat rows 4 and 5 once more.
Row 8: Purl to last stitch, m1, p1—18 stitches.
Row 9: K1, m1, knit to end—19 stitches.
Repeat rows 8 and 9 once more.
Row 12: Purl to last stitch, m1, p1—
22 stitches.
Row 13: Knit.
Row 14: Purl.
Repeat rows 13 and 14 twice more.
Next row: Bind off 5 stitches, knit to end—
17 stitches.
Next row: Purl to last 3 stitches, p2tog, p1—
16 stitches.
Next row: Bind off 4 stitches, knit to end—
12 stitches.
Next row: Purl.
Next row: Knit.
Next row: P1, p2tog, purl to last 3 stitches,
p2tog, p1—10 stitches.
Next row: K1, k2tog, knit to last 3 stitches,
k2tog, k1—8 stitches.
Bind off.

GUSSET
Using size 3 (3.25mm) needles, cast on
4 stitches.
Row 1: Knit.
Row 2: Purl.
Row 3: K1, m1, k1, m1, k1, m1, k1—7 stitches.
Row 4: Purl.
Row 5: K1, m1, knit to last stitch, m1, k1—
9 stitches.
Repeat rows 4 and 5 twice more—13 stitches.
Row 10: Purl.
Row 11: Knit.
Row 12: Purl.
Row 13: K1, m1, knit to last stitch, m1, k1—
15 stitches.
Row 14: Purl.
Row 15: Knit.

Row 16: Purl.
Row 17: Knit.
Row 18: Purl.
Row 19: K1, m1, knit to last stitch, m1, k1—
17 stitches.
Row 20: Purl.
Row 21: Knit.
Row 22: Purl.
Row 23: Knit.
Row 24: Purl.
Row 25: K2tog, knit to last 2 stitches, k2tog—
15 stitches.
Row 26: Purl.
Row 27: K2tog, knit to last 2 stitches, k2tog—
13 stitches.
Repeat rows 26 and 27 until 9 stitches remain.
Row 32: Purl.
Row 33: Knit.
Repeat rows 32 and 33 4 more times.
Row 42: Purl.
Row 43: K2tog, knit to last 2 stitches, k2tog—
7 stitches.
Row 44: Purl.
Repeat rows 43 and 44 twice more—3 stitches.
Next row: Sl2, k1, p2sso.
Fasten off.

LEGS (MAKE 2)
Using size 3 (3.25mm) needles, cast on
17 stitches.
Row 1: Knit.
Row 2: Purl.
Row 3: K1, m1, knit to last stitch, m1, k1—19
stitches.
Repeat rows 2 and 3 once more—21 stitches.
Row 6: Purl.
Row 7: Knit.
Row 8: Purl.
Repeat rows 7 and 8 5 more times.
Row 19: K8, k2togtbl, k1, k2tog, k8—19
stitches.

Row 20: Purl.
Row 21: Knit.
Row 22: Purl.
Row 23: K9, m1, k1, m1, k9—21 stitches.
Row 24: P10, m1, p1, m1, p10—23 stitches.
Repeat rows 23 and 24 until there are 31
stitches.
Row 29: Knit.
Row 30: Purl.
Row 31: Knit.
Bind off.

FEET PADS (MAKE 2)
Using size 3 (3.25mm) needles, cast on
3 stitches. Work as for knitting the feet pads
on page 64.

ARMS (MAKE 4 PIECES)
Using size 3 (3.25mm) needles, cast on
3 stitches. Work as for knitting the inner arms
until * on page 64.
Repeat rows 7 and 8 12 more times, and then
row 7 again.
Row 32: K1, k2tog, k3, k2tog, k1—7 stitches.
Row 33: Purl.
Row 34: K1, k2tog, k1, k2tog, k1—5 stitches.
Do not bind off. Thread yarn through the
remaining stitches and pull together to secure.

EARS (MAKE 2)
Using size 3 (3.25mm) needles, cast on
7 stitches.

Row 1: Knit.
Row 2: K1, p5, k1.
Repeat rows 1 and 2 once more.
Row 5: K2tog, knit to last 2 stitches, k2tog—
5 stitches.
Bind off and, **at the same time**, k2tog at each
end of the bind-off row. Leave a long enough
thread to shape the ear and to it attach to the
head.

FINISHING
HEAD
Starting at the cast-on edges, sew together the
gusset and left side of head until you reach the
tip of the snout. Attach the right side of the
head in the same way.

Starting at the tip of the snout, continue
sewing the seam until you are ⅔ of the way
along the 2 cast-on edges of the sides. Using
the opening that you have left, stuff the head
until it is firm (using the photograph as a guide
to help you to achieve a good shape). Finally,
weave the yarn around the side of the opening
and pull, gathering the seams together (like a
drawstring). Fasten securely.

Facial features
Using the brown yarn (Rowan Calmer shade
481), sew the bear's facial features as follows:

Eyes
Measure approximately 1⅝" (4cm) up each
gusset seam from the tip of the snout. Using a
long sewing needle, create each eye as
described under finishing the eyes, from *, on
page 64.

Nose and Mouth
Work as for finishing the nose and mouth on
page 65, only making the long single vertical
stitch ⅜" (0.75cm) long.

BODY
Work as for finishing the body on page 65.

ARMS
Each arm is made up of two pieces. Join the
2 pieces starting at the top of the arm, working
down one side and then up the other, leaving
an opening for stuffing. Stuff the arm, then
fasten securely.

LEGS
Work as for finishing the legs on page 65.

EARS
Mark the position of the ears as follows:
Measure approximately 2⅜" (6cm) from the tip
of the snout. Work as for finishing the ears,
from *, on page 65.

ASSEMBLING YOUR BEAR
Work as for assembling the bear on page 65.

Hula Bear

Hula Bear can't wait to dance you away to exotic locations. Put a flower in her hair and she's ready to go!

SKILL LEVEL
Simple

MATERIALS
For the skirt
- 118 yds (108m) sport weight yarn **2** fine (A). The bear's outfit on page 38 uses 1 skein Rowan Summer Tweed, 70% silk, 30% cotton, 1 oz (50g), 118 yds (108m), 507 Rush

For the top
- 126 yds (115m) sport weight yarn **2** fine (B). The bear's outfit on page 38 uses 1 ball Rowan Cotton Glace, 100% cotton, 1 oz (50g), 137 yds (115m), 809 Pier

For the flowers
- 126 yds (115m) sport weight yarn **2** fine in 3 shades—2 appropriate for flowers (C and D) and 1 appropriate for leaves (E). The bear's outfit on page 38 uses small amounts Rowan Cotton Glace, 741 Poppy (C), 832 Persimmon (D), 812 Ivy (E)
- 1 7mm snap
- Sizes 3 and 7 (3.25mm and 4.5mm) needles (or size needed to obtain gauge)

GAUGE
SKIRT
16 stitches and 23 rows to 4" (10cm) using size 7 (4.5mm) needles and sport weight yarn, measured over stockinette stitch.

TOP
23 stitches and 32 rows to 4" (10cm) using size 3 (3.25mm) needles and sport weight yarn, measured over stockinette stitch.

SKIRT

Using size 7 (4.5mm) needles and A, cast on 17 stitches.

Row 1: *Bind off 13 stitches, k4.

Row 2: Turn and k4, turn and cast on 13 stitches.

Repeat rows 1 and 2 until 19 sections have been worked, finishing with binding off 13 stitches, k4.

Next 4 rows: Knit.

Bind off.

TOP

Using size 3 (3.25mm) needles and B, cast on 44 stitches.

Row 1: Knit.

Row 2: Purl.

Repeat rows 1 and 2 4 more times.

Bind off.

Flowers (make 2 in C and 1 in D)

Using size 3 (3.25mm) needles, cast on 23 stitches.

Row 1: K1, *k2, lift the first of these 2 stitches over the second, repeat from * to end—12 stitches.

Row 2: P1, (p2tog) to end—6 stitches. Do not bind off. Thread the yarn through the remaining stitches, then pull together.

Leaves (make 2)

Using size 3 (3.25mm) needles and E, cast on 3 stitches.

Row 1: K1, p1, k1.

Row 2: K1, m1, k1, m1, k1—5 stitches.

Row 3: K1, p3, k1.

Row 4: K2, m1, k1, m1, k2—7 stitches.

Row 5: K1, p5, k1.

Row 6: K2, sl2, k1, p2sso, k2—5 stitches.

Row 7: K1, p3, k1.

Row 8: K1, sl2, k1, p2sso, k1—3 stitches.

Row 9: Sl2, k1, p2sso—1 stitch.

Fasten off.

FINISHING

SKIRT

The skirt has been knitted all in 1 piece. Sew the snap onto the inside of the waistband at the bound-off end. Sew the other half of the snap button to the corresponding position on the outside of the waistband at the cast-on end.

TOP

The top has been knitted all in 1 piece. Sew the 2 sides together, creating a seam at the center back.

FLOWERS

Using the photograph as a guide, stitch a red flower, a yellow flower, and 2 leaves to the front left-hand side of the skirt waistband. Pin a red flower behind the bear's ear.

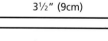

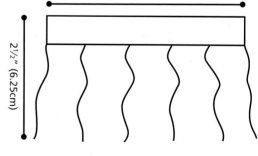

3½" (9cm)

1¼" (3cm)

4" (10cm)

2½" (6.25cm)

Robin Hood Bear

Ready to steal from the rich and give to the poor, Robin Hood Bear strides across Sherwood Forest with his quiver of arrows. With a jaunty hat and sturdy boots, he's sure to be everyone's hero.

SKILL LEVEL
Intermediate

MATERIALS

For the tunic

- 142 yds (130m) DK weight yarn 3 light (A). The bear's outfit on page 40 uses 1 ball Rowan Classic Cashsoft DK, 57% extra fine merino, 33% microfiber, 10% cashmere, 1 oz (50g), 142 yds (130m), 523 Lichen

For the boots

- 142 yds (130m) DK weight yarn 3 light (B). The bear's outfit on page 40 uses 1 ball Rowan Classic Cashsoft DK, 522 Cashew

For the tights and quiver

- 142 yds (130m) DK weight yarn 3 light (C). The bear's outfit on page 40 uses 1 ball Rowan Classic Cashsoft DK, 517 Donkey
- 20" (51cm) brown leather lace
- Sizes 3 and 6 (3.25mm and 4mm) needles (or size needed to obtain gauge)
- 20" (51cm) brown leather lace
- Tapestry needle
- Toothpicks

GAUGE

TIGHTS

23 stitches and 36 rows to 4" (10cm) using size 3 (3.25mm) needles and DK weight yarn, measured over stockinette stitch.

TUNIC

22 stitches and 30 rows to 4" (10cm) using size 6 (4mm) needles and DK weight yarn, measured over stockinette stitch.

BOOTS

22 stitches and 30 rows to 4" (10cm) using size 6 (4mm) needles and DK weight yarn, measured over stockinette stitch.

TIGHTS

Front

Leg (make 2)

Using size 3 (3.25mm) needles and C, cast on 13 stitches.

Row 1: K1, (p1, k1) to end.
Row 2: P1, (k1, p1) to end.
Row 3: K1, (p1, k1) to end.
Row 4: Purl.
Row 5: Knit.
Row 6: Purl.

Repeat rows 5 and 6 9 more times, ending with a wrong-side row.

Do not bind off. Leave the stitches on a holder. Join the 2 legs of the front section as follows: With right-sides facing, knit across 12 of the 13 stitches of left leg, knit the last stitch of the left leg together with the first stitch of the right leg, knit to end—25 stitches.

Next row: Purl.
Next row: Knit.
Next row: Purl.
Repeat the last 2 rows 7 more times.
Bind off.

Back

Work the same as for the Front.

TUNIC

Zigzag edging

Make 6 triangles as follows:
Using size 6 (4mm) needles and A, cast on 1 stitch.

Row 1: Increase in first stitch—2 stitches.
Row 2: Increase purlwise into first stitch, purl to end—3 stitches.
Row 3: Increase knitwise into first stitch, knit to end—4 stitches.
Row 4: Increase purlwise into first stitch, purl to end—5 stitches.
Row 5: Increase knitwise into first stitch, knit to end—6 stitches.
Row 6: Increase purlwise into first stitch, purl to end—7 stitches.
Row 7: Increase knitwise into first stitch, knit to end—8 stitches.
Row 8: Increase purlwise into first stitch, purl to end—9 stitches.
Row 9: Knit.
Do not bind off. Leave the stitches on a holder. Repeat until you have 6 triangles on holders.

Front

Join 3 of the triangles as follows: With wrong sides facing, purl across 9 stitches of one triangle, 9 stitches of second triangle, and then

9 stitches of third triangle—27 stitches.
Row 2: Knit.
Row 3: Purl.
Row 4: Knit.
Row 5: Purl.
Row 6: K3, k3tog, (k6, k3tog) to last 3 stitches, k3—21 stitches.
Row 7: Purl.
Row 8: Knit.
Row 9: Purl.
Repeat rows 8 and 9 8 more times, ending with a wrong-side row.

Shape front neck

Row 26: K10, turn and work as follows:
Row 27: K1, p9.
Row 28: K to last 3 stitches, k2tog, k1—9 stitches.
Row 29: K1, purl to end.
Row 30: Knit.
Row 31: K1, purl to end.
Row 32: Knit to last 3 stitches, k2tog, k1—8 stitches.
Repeat rows 29 through 32 twice more—6 stitches.
Row 41: K1, p5.

Row 42: Knit.
Row 43: K1, p5.
Do not bind off. Leave the shoulder stitches on a holder.

Shape right neck

Row 26: Rejoing the yarn to the remaining stitches, bind off the center stitch and knit to the end—10 stitches.
Row 27: P9, k1.
Row 28: K1, k2togtbl, knit to end—9 stitches.
Row 29: Purl to last stitch, k1.
Row 30: Knit.
Row 31: Purl to last stitch, k1.
Row 32: K1, k2togtbl, knit to end—8 stitches.
Repeat rows 29 through 32 twice more—6 stitches.
Row 41: P5, k1.
Row 42: Knit.
Row 43: P5, k1.
Do not bind off. Leave the shoulder stitches on a holder.

Back

Work rows 1 through 6 of the Front (page 40).
Row 7: Purl.
Row 8: Knit.
Row 9: Purl.
Repeat rows 8 and 9 16 more times, ending with a wrong-side row.
Next row: Knit.
Next row: P6, bind off center 9 stitches, k6.
Do not bind off. Leave the 2 sets of shoulder stitches on a holder.

SLEEVES

Zigzag edging

Make 8 triangles as follows:
Using size 6 (4mm) needles and A, cast on 1 stitch.
Row 1: Increase in first stitch—2 stitches.
Row 2: Increase purlwise into first stitch, purl to end—3 stitches.
Row 3: Increase knitwise into first stitch, knit to end—4 stitches.
Row 4: Increase purlwise into first stitch, purl to end—5 stitches.
Row 5: Increase knitwise into first stitch, knit to end—6 stitches.
Row 6: Purl.
Do not bind off. Leave stitches on a holder.
Repeat until you have 8 triangles on holders.

Sleeves (make 2)

Join 4 of the triangles as follows: With right sides facing, knit across 6 stitches of one triangle, 6 stitches of a second triangle, 6 stitches of a third triangle, and 6 stitches of a fourth triangle—24 stitches.
Row 2: Purl.
Row 3: K2, k2tog, (k4, k2tog) to last 2 stitches, k2—20 stitches.
Row 4: Purl.
Row 5: Knit.
Row 6: Purl.
Repeat rows 5 and 6 3 more times, ending with a wrong-side row.
Bind off.

BOOTS (MAKE 2)

Using size 6 (4mm) needles and B, cast on 21 stitches.
Row 1: Knit.
Row 2: Purl.
Repeat rows 1 and 2 once more.
Row 5: Purl. (This reverses the stockinette stitch.)
Row 6: Knit.
Repeat rows 5 and 6 6 more times.
Row 19: Purl.
Row 20: K8, k2togtbl, k1, k2tog, k8—19 stitches.
Row 21: Purl.
Row 22: Knit.

Row 23: Purl.
Row 24: K9, m1, k1, m1, k9—21 stitches.
Row 25: P10, m1, p1, m1, p10—23 stitches.
Repeat rows 24 and 25 until there are 31 stitches.
Row 30: Knit.
Row 31: Purl.
Row 32: Knit.
Bind off.

Soles (make 2)

Using size 6 (4mm) needles and B, cast on 3 stitches.
Row 1: Purl.
Row 2: K1, m1, k1, m1, k1—5 stitches.
Row 3: Purl.
Row 4: K1, m1, knit to last stitch, m1, k1—7 stitches.
Repeat rows 3 and 4 once more—9 stitches.
Row 7: Purl.
Row 8: Knit.
Row 9: Purl.
Repeat rows 8 and 9 twice more.
Row 14: K2, k2tog, k1, k2tog, k2—7 stitches.
Row 15: Purl.
Row 16: K1, k2tog, k1, k2tog, k1—5 stitches.
Bind off and, **at the same time**, k2tog at each end of the bound-off row.

QUIVER

Using size 3 (3.25mm) needles and C, cast on 4 stitches.

Row 1: Purl.
Row 2: K1, (m1, k1) to end—7 stitches.
Row 3: Purl.
Row 4: K1, m1, k5, m1, k1—9 stitches.
Row 5: Purl.
Row 6: K1, m1, k7, m1, k1—11 stitches.
Row 7: Purl.
Row 8: K1, m1, k9, m1, k1—13 stitches.
Row 9: Purl.
Row 10: K1, m1, k11, m1, k1—15 stitches.
Row 11: Purl.
Row 12: Knit.
Row 13: Purl.
Repeat rows 12 and 13 4 more times, ending with a wrong-side row.
Bind off.

HAT

Left side

Using size 3 (3.25mm) needles and A, cast on

15 stitches.

Row 1: Knit.
Row 2: Purl.
Row 3: Knit to last 2 stitches, k2tog—14 stitches.
Row 4: Purl.
Repeat rows 3 and 4 until 12 stitches remain.
Next row: Knit to last 2 stitches, k2tog—11 stitches.
Next row: P2tog, purl to end—10 stitches.
Repeat the last 2 rows until 6 stitches remain.
Bind off.

Right side

Using size 3 (3.25mm) needles and A, cast on 15 stitches.

Row 1: Knit.
Row 2: Purl.
Row 3: K2tog, knit to end—14 stitches.
Row 4: Purl.
Repeat the last 2 rows until 12 stitches remain.
Next row: K2tog, knit to end—11 stitches.
Next row: Purl to last 2 stitches, p2tog—10 stitches.
Repeat the last 2 rows until 6 stitches remain.
Bind off.

Back section

Using size 3 (3.25mm) needles and A, cast on 7 stitches.

Row 1: Knit.
Row 2: Purl.
Repeat rows 1 and 2 twice more, ending with a wrong-side row.
Next row: K2tog, knit to last 2 stitches, k2tog—5 stitches.
Next row: Purl.
Next row: K2tog, k1, k2tog—3 stitches.
Next row: Purl.
Next row: Sl2, k1, p2sso.
Fasten off.

FINISHING

TIGHTS

Join front and back of the tights as follows: Sew the outer side seams—start at top (bound-off edge) and work down to the bottom (cast-on edge). Now join the inner-leg seams. Starting at the cast-on edge of the right leg, work up to the top, and then work down the corresponding seam of the left leg.

TUNIC

Join shoulder seams using the three-needle bind-off as described on page 26.

Sleeves

Fold each sleeve in half lengthwise and mark the center of the bound-off edge with a stitch marker. Line this marker up with the shoulder seam and tack the sleeve in place. Then sew the sleeve to the body. Attach both sleeves in the same way.

Join both side and sleeve seams.

HAT

Join the left and right sides by sewing the 2 shaped edges together. Then, sew the left edge of the back section to the straight edge of the left side, and the right edge of the back section to the straight edge of the right side. The cast-on edge of the 2 side edges will naturally curl, and this creates the brim.

BOOTS

Fold the boot in half lengthwise and, starting at row 5 (where the stockinette stitch has been reversed), sew the 2 side edges together to form a seam which runs down the back of the boot. Attach the sole by sewing around the edges of the sole, and joining it to the bound-off edge of the boot. Fold down the top part of the boot.

QUIVER

Fold the quiver in half lengthwise and sew the 2 side edges together, forming a seam that runs down the back of the quiver. Using the photograph as a guide, thread a length of leather lace through the top of the quiver as follows: Using a tapestry needle, thread the leather in through the quiver just to the right of the seam, and then back out just to the left of the seam. Leave long lengths and tie in a knot. The quiver can then be carried over the bear's shoulder. Fill the quiver with toothpick arrows.

BELT

Using the photograph as a guide, tie a length of leather strip lace around the waist and tie in a knot.

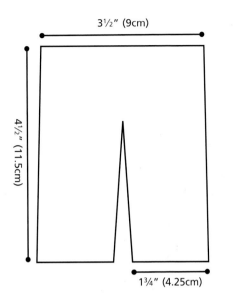

3½" (9cm)

4½" (11.5cm)

1¾" (4.25cm)

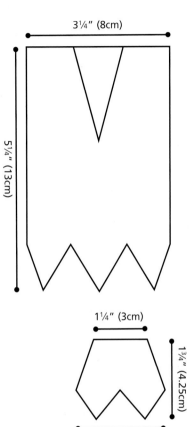

3¼" (8cm)

5¼" (13cm)

1¼" (3cm)

1¾" (4.25cm)

2" (5cm)

Cheerleader Bear

With her cute little pom-poms and uniform, Cheerleader Bear will lend her support to your school or favorite sports team. Why not dress her in your team colors?

SKILL LEVEL
Simple

MATERIALS
For the skirt and sweater
- 93 yds (85m) worsted weight yarn (4) medium (A). The bear's outfit opposite uses 1 ball Rowan Handknit Cotton, 100% cotton, 1 oz (50g), 93 yds (85m), 263 Bleached

For the skirt, sweater and pom-poms
- 93 yds (85m) worsted weight yarn (4) medium (B). The bear's outfit opposite uses 1 ball Rowan Handknit Cotton, 305 Lupin
- Sizes 3 and 6 (3.25mm and 4mm) needles (or size needed to obtain gauge)
- Tapestry needle

GAUGE
20 stitches and 28 rows to 4" (10cm) using size 6 (4mm) needles and worsted weight yarn measured over stockinette stitch.

SKIRT
Using size 3 (3.25mm) needles and A, cast on 46 stitches.
Change to yarn B.
Row 1: Knit.
Row 2: Purl.
Change to yarn A.
Row 3: Knit.
Row 4: Purl.
Row 6: Knit.
Row 7: Purl.
Row 8: K3, k2tog, (k4, k2tog) to last 3 stitches, k3—37 stitches.
Row 9: Purl.

Row 10: K2, k2tog, k3, (k2tog, k3) to end—30 stitches.
Row 11: Purl.
Row 12: K2, (k2tog, k2) to end—23 stitches.
Row 13: Purl.
Row 14: K2, k2tog, knit to last 4 stitches, k2tog, k2—21 stitches.
Row 15: Purl.
Row 16: Knit.
Row 17: Purl.
Row 18: Knit.
Bind off.

SWEATER
Back
Using size 3 (3.25mm) needles and A, cast on 23 stitches.
Row 1: (K1, p1) to last stitch, k1.
Row 2: (P1, k1) to last stitch, p1.
Change to yarn B.
Row 3: Knit.
Change to yarn A.
Row 4: Purl.
Row 5: Knit.
Row 6: Purl.
Repeat rows 5 and 6 10 more times.
Next row: K5, bind off center 13 stitches, k5.
Do not bind off. Leave the shoulder stitches on a holder.
With right side facing, rejoin yarn to one set of the remaining 5 stitches and work as follows:
Next row: Purl.
Next row: Knit.
Do not bind off. Leave the shoulder stitches on a holder.
Repeat for the other shoulder.

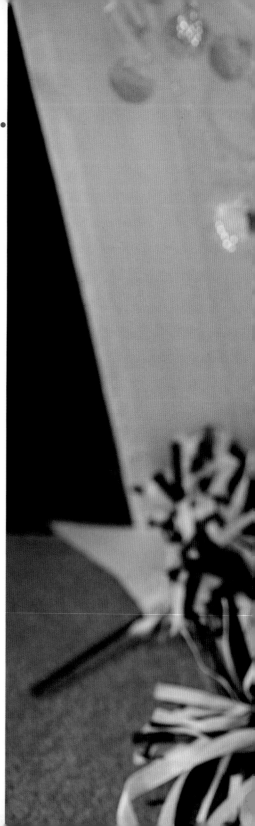

Front

Using size 3 (3.25mm) needles and A, cast on 23 stitches.

Row 1: (K1, p1) to last stitch, k1.

Row 2: (P1, k1) to last stitch, p1.

Change to yarn B.

Row 3: Knit.

Change to yarn A.

Row 4: Purl.

Row 5: Knit.

Row 6: Purl.

Repeat rows 5 and 6 4 more times.

Row 11: K11, turn and work on these 11 stitches only as follows:

Row 12: Bind off 1 stitch, purl to end— 10 stitches.

Row 13: Knit to last 3 stitches, k2tog, k1—9 stitches.

Row 14: Purl.

Row 15: Knit to last 3 stitches, k2tog, k1—8 stitches.

Repeat last 2 rows 3 more times—5 stitches.

Row 19: Purl.

Do not bind off. Leave the shoulder stitches on a holder.

With right side facing, rejoin yarn to the remaining stitches and work as follows:

Row 20: Bind off next stitch, knit to end— 11 stitches.

Row 21: Purl to last 3 stitches, p2togtbl, p1— 10 stitches.

Row 22: K1, k2togtbl, knit to end— 9 stitches.

Row 23: Purl.

Row 24: K1, k2togtbl, knit to end— 8 stitches.

Repeat last 2 rows 3 more times—5 stitches.

Row 28: Purl.

Do not bind off. Break yarn and leave the shoulder stitches on a holder.

SLEEVES (MAKE 2)

Using size 3 (3.25mm) needles and A, cast on 46 stitches.

Row 1: (K1, p1) to end.

Repeat last row once more.

Change to yarn B.

Row 3: Knit.

Change to yarn A.

Row 4: Purl.

Row 5: Knit.

Row 6: Purl.

Repeat rows 5 and 6 3 more times.

Bind off.

FINISHING

SKIRT

The skirt has been knitted in 2 pieces. Sew together the 2 side seams.

SWEATER

Join the right shoulder seam using the three-needle bind-off technique as described on page 26.

With right sides facing and using B and size 3 (3.25mm) needles, pick up and knit 13 stitches down the right front of the neck, 13 stitches up the left front of the neck, and 14 stitches from the back of the neck—40 stitches. Bind off.

Join left shoulder, using the three-needle bind-off technique as described on page 26.

Sleeves

Fold sleeve in half lengthwise and mark the center of the bound-off edge with a stitch marker. Line this marker up with the shoulder seam and tack the sleeve in place. Now sew the sleeve to the body. Attach both sleeves in the same way.

Join both side and sleeve seams.

POM-POMS

Using B, make 2 pom-poms as follows: Cut 2 circles of card approximately ¾" (2cm) in diameter with a ⅜" (1cm)-diameter hole in the middle. Wind the yarn around the outside of the 2 circles of card until the hole in the center is almost filled in. Next, cut slowly and carefully around the edges of the 2 pieces of card until all the yarn has been cut. Gently ease the pieces of card apart, **but before taking them off completely**, tie a piece of yarn in a secure knot around the center of the pom-pom to hold it together. Now remove the card. Attach a loop of yarn to each pom-pom, big enough to fit around the bear's arms.

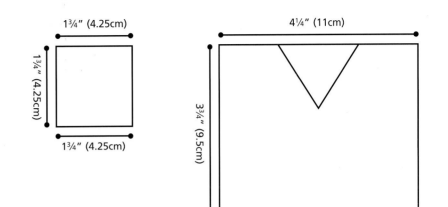

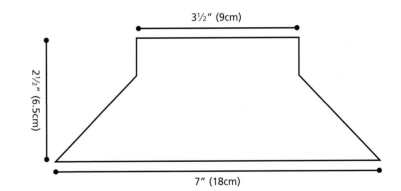

Intermediate Large Bear

This large bear is the perfect size for hugging! Kids and adults will just love this nearly 14" tall bear—and with so many outfits to choose from, you could spend hours playing dress-up!

FINISHED SIZE
Height: 13¾" (35cm)
Diameter (around body): 12¾" (30cm)

MATERIALS
Option A (Beige)
- 142 yds (130m) DK weight yarn. **3**
  The bear on page 57 uses 2 balls Rowan Classic Cashsoft DK, 57% extra fine merino, 33% microfiber, 10% cashmere, 1 oz (50g), 142 yds (130m), 507 Savannah

Option B (Tweed)
- 142 yds (130m) DK weight yarn. **3**
  The bear on page 55 uses 2 balls Rowan Scottish Tweed DK, 100% wool, 1 oz (50g), 142 yds (130m), 025 Oatmeal
- Size 5 (3.75mm) needles (or size needed to obtain gauge)
- 175 yds (160m) sport weight yarn **3** light for facial features. The bear on page 55 uses small amount Rowan Calmer, 75% cotton, 25% acrylic, 1 oz (50g), 124 yds (113m), 481 Coffee Bean
- Tapestry needle
- 3oz (85g) toy stuffing

GAUGE
24 stitches and 32 rows to 4" (10cm) using size 5 (3.75mm) needles and DK weight yarn, measured over stockinette stitch.

BODY
Sides (make 2)
Using size 5 (3.75mm) needles, cast on 11 stitches.

Row 1 (RS): Knit.
Row 2: Purl.
Row 3: K5, m1, k1, m1, k5—13 stitches.
Row 4: Purl.
Keeping shaping as set (increasing on either side of the center stitch), repeat rows 3 and 4 until there are 31 stitches.
Row 23: Knit.
Row 24: Purl.
Repeat rows 23 and 24 12 more times, ending with a wrong-side row.
Row 49: K11, (k2togtbl) twice, k1 (k2tog) twice, knit to end—27 stitches.
Row 50: Purl.
Row 51: K9, (k2togtbl) twice, k1 (k2tog) twice, knit to end—23 stitches.
Row 52: P9, p2tog, p1, p2togtbl, purl to end—21 stitches.
Row 53: K8, k2togtbl, k1, k2tog, knit to end—19 stitches.
Row 54: P7, p2tog, p1, p2togtbl, purl to end—17 stitches.
Row 55: K6, k2togtbl, k1 k2tog, knit to end—15 stitches.
Row 56: P5, p2tog, p1 p2togtbl, purl to end—13 stitches.
Row 57: (P2tog) 3 times, p1, (p2tog) to end—7 stitches.
Do not bind off. Thread yarn through the remaining stitches and pull together to secure.

HEAD
Right side
Using size 5 (3.75mm) needles, cast on 17 stitches.
Row 1: Knit.
Row 2: Purl.
Repeat rows 1 and 2 once more.
Row 5: K1, m1, knit to last stitch, m1, k1—19 stitches.
Row 6: Purl.
Repeat rows 5 and 6 once more—21 stitches.
Row 9: Knit.
Row 10: Purl to last stitch, m1, p1—22 stitches.
Row 11: K1, m1, knit to end—23 stitches.
Row 12: Purl to last stitch, m1, p1—24 stitches.
Row 13: K1, m1, knit to end—25 stitches.
Row 14: Purl to last stitch, m1, p1—26 stitches.
Row 15: Knit.
Row 16: Purl.
Row 17: Knit.
Row 18: Purl.
Row 19: Knit.
Row 20: Purl.
Row 21: Knit.
Row 22: Purl.
Row 23: Bind off 6 stitches, knit to end—20 stitches.
Row 24: Purl to last 3 stitches, p2tog, p1—19 stitches.
Row 25: Knit.
Row 26: Purl.
Row 27: Bind off 5 stitches, knit to end—14 stitches.
Row 28: Purl.
Row 29: Knit.
Row 30: Purl.
Row 31: Knit.
Row 32: Purl.

Row 33: K1, k2tog, knit to last 3 stitches, k2tog, k1—12 stitches.
Row 34: P1, p2tog, purl to last 3 stitches, p2tog, p1—10 stitches.
Bind off.

Left side

Using size 5 (3.75mm) needles, cast on 17 stitches.
Row 1: Knit.
Row 2: Purl.
Row 3: Knit.
Row 4: P1, m1, purl to last stitch, m1, p1—19 stitches.
Row 5: Knit.
Repeat rows 4 and 5 once more—21 stitches.
Row 8: Purl.
Row 9: Knit to last stitch, m1, k1—22 stitches.
Row 10: P1, m1, purl to end—23 stitches.
Row 11: Knit to last stitch, m1, k1—24 stitches.
Row 12: P1, m1, purl to end—25 stitches.
Row 13: Knit to last stitch, m1, k1—26 stitches.
Row 14: Purl.
Row 15: Knit.
Row 16: Purl.
Row 17: Knit.
Row 18: Purl.
Row 19: Knit.
Row 20: Purl.
Row 21: Knit.
Row 22: Bind off 6 stitches, purl to end—20 stitches.
Row 23: Knit to last 3 stitches, k2tog, k1—19 stitches.
Row 24: Purl.
Row 25: Knit.
Row 26: Bind off 5 stitches, purl to end—14 stitches.
Row 27: Knit.

Row 28: Purl.
Row 29: Knit.
Row 30: Purl.
Row 31: Knit.
Row 32: P1, p2tog, purl to last 3 stitches, p2tog, p1—12 stitches.
Row 33: K1, k2tog, knit to last 3 stitches, k2tog, k1—10 stitches.
Bind off.

Head gusset

Using size 5 (3.75mm) needles, cast on 5 stitches.
Row 1: Knit.
Row 2: Purl.
Row 3: K1, m1, k1, m1, k1, m1, k1, m1, k1—9 stitches.
Row 4: Purl.
Row 5: K1, m1, knit to last stitch, m1, k1—11 stitches.
Repeat rows 4 and 5 twice more—15 stitches.
Row 10: Purl.
Row 11: Knit.
Row 12: Purl.
Row 13: K1, m1, knit to last stitch, m1, k1—17 stitches.
Row 14: Purl.
Row 15: Knit.
Row 16: Purl.
Row 17: Knit.
Row 18: Purl.
Row 19: Knit.
Row 20: Purl.
Row 21: K1, m1, knit to last stitch, m1, k1—19 stitches.
Row 22: Purl.
Row 23: Knit.
Row 24: Purl.
Row 25: Knit.
Row 26: Purl.
Row 27: Knit.

Row 28: Purl.
Row 29: Knit.
Row 30: Purl.
Row 31: K2tog, knit to last 2 stitches, k2tog—17 stitches.
Row 32: Purl.
Row 33: K2tog, knit to last 2 stitches, k2tog—15 stitches.
Repeat rows 32 and 33 until 9 stitches remain.
Next row: Purl.
Next row: Knit.
Repeat the last 2 rows 4 more times.
Next row: Purl.
Next row: K2tog, knit to last 2 stitches, k2tog—7 stitches.
Next row: Purl.
Repeat the last 2 rows twice more.
Next row: Sl2, k1, p2sso.
Fasten off.

LEGS (MAKE 2)

Using size 5 (3.75mm) needles, cast on 19 stitches.
Row 1: Knit.
Row 2: Purl.
Row 3: K1, m1, knit to last stitch, m1, k1—21 stitches.
Repeat rows 2 and 3 once more—23 stitches.
Row 6: Purl
Row 7: Knit.

Row 8: Purl.

Repeat rows 7 and 8 8 more times.

Row 25: K9, k2togtbl, k1, k2tog, k9—21 stitches.

Row 26: P8, p2tog, p1, p2togtbl, p8—19 stitches.

Row 27: Knit.

Row 28: Purl.

Row 29: K9, m1, k1, m1, k9—21 stitches.

Row 30: P10, m1, p1, m1, p10—23 stitches.

Keeping shaping as set (increasing on either side of the center stitch), repeat rows 29 and 30 until there are 31 stitches.

Next row: Knit.

Next row: Purl.

Next row: Knit.

Next row: Purl.

Next row: Knit.

Bind off.

FEET PADS (MAKE 2)

Using size 5 (3.75mm) needles, cast on 4 stitches.

Row 1: Purl.

Row 2: K1, (m1, k1) to end—7 stitches.

Row 3: Purl.

Row 4: K1, m1, knit to last stitch, m1, k1 —9 stitches.

Repeat rows 3 and 4 once more—11 stitches.

Next row: Purl.

Next row: Knit.

Next row: Purl.

Repeat the last 2 rows 3 more times.

Next row: K2, k2tog, k3, k2tog, k2—9 stitches.

Next row: Purl.

Next row: K2, k2tog, k1, k2tog, k2—7 stitches.

Bind off and, **at the same time**, k2tog at each end of bind-off row.

ARMS (MAKE 4)

Using size 5 (3.75mm) needles, cast on 4 stitches.

Row 1: Purl.

Row 2: K1 (m1, k1) to end—7 stitches.

Row 3: Purl.

Row 4: K1, m1, k5, m1, k1—9 stitches.

Row 5: Purl.

Row 6: K1, m1, k7, m1, k1—11 stitches.

Row 7: Purl.

Row 8: Knit.

Repeat rows 7 and 8 14 more times, and then row 7 once more.

Next row: K1, k2tog, k5, k2tog, k1—9 stitches.

Next row: Purl.

Next row: K1, k2tog, k3, k2tog, k1—7 stitches.

Do not bind off. Thread yarn through the remaining stitches and pull together to secure.

EARS (MAKE 2)

Using size 3 (3.25mm) needles cast on 9 stitches.

Row 1: Knit.

Row 2: K1, p7, k1.

Rep rows 1 and 2 once more.

Row 5: K2tog, knit to last 2 stitches, k2tog—7 stitches.

Row 6: P2tog, purl to last 2 stitches, p2tog—5 stitches.

Bind off and, **at the same time**, k2tog at each end of bind-off row. Leave a long enough thread to shape ear and attach it to the head.

FINISHING

HEAD

Work as for finishing the head on page 36.

FACIAL FEATURES

Using the brown yarn (Rowan Calmer shade 481), sew the bear's facial features as follows:

Eyes

Work as for finishing the eyes on page 64.

Nose and mouth

Work as for finishing the nose and mouth on page 65, but make the single vertical stitch ⅝" (1.5cm) long, and the 2 diagonal stitches ¼" (0.75cm) long.

BODY

Work as for finishing the body on page 65, stuffing the bear to approximately 11¾" (30cm) in diameter.

ARMS

Work as for finishing the arms on page 36.

LEGS

Work as for finishing the legs on page 65.

EARS

Mark the position of the ears as follows: Measure approximately 3¼" (8cm) from the tip of the snout. Work as for finishing the ears from * on page 65.

Using the long tail that you left when binding off, give the ear some shape by sewing the tail around the outer edge of the ear, then using the same thread to attach to the head.

ASSEMBLING THE BEAR

Work as for assembling the bear on page 65, but sew the legs approximately ¾" (2cm) from the beginning of the side shaping.

Fisherman Bear

With his hat, cable-knit sweater, and a cute little fish on the end of his line, Fisherman Bear is quite a catch. Any fishing fan would be delighted to get Fisherman Bear as a gift—if you can part with him!

SKILL LEVEL
Intermediate

MATERIALS

For the sweater
- 137 yds (125m) DK weight yarn (3) light
  (A). The bear's outfit on page 55 uses 1 ball
  Rowan Pure Wool DK, 100% wool, 1 oz
  (50g), 136 yds (125m), shade 0121 Glade

For the pants
- 142 yds (130m) DK weight yarn (3) light
  (B). The bear's outfit on page 55 uses 1 ball
  Rowan Classic Cashsoft DK, 57% extra fine
  merino, 33% microfiber, 10% cashmere,
  1 oz (50g), 142 yds (130m), 522 Cashew

For the rain boots and hat
- 123 yds (113m) DK weight yarn (3) light
  (C). The bear's outfit on page 55 uses 1 ball
  Rowan Wool Cotton, 50% wool, 50%
  cotton, 1 oz (50g), 123 yds (113m), 907
  Deepest Olive

For the fish
- 126 yds (115m) sport weight yarn (2) fine
  for the fish (D). The bear's outfit on page 55
  uses small amount Rowan Cotton Glace,
  100% cotton, 1 oz (50g), 137 yds (115m),
  832 Persimmon
- Sizes 3 and 6 (3.25mm and 4mm) needles
  (or size needed to obtain gauge)
- 2 10mm buttons, such as Rowan 00408
- 2 7mm snaps
- Thin wooden doweling, approximately
  10" (25cm) long
- Black sewing thread
- Sewing needle
- 4" (10cm) 28 gauge craft wire
- Cable needle

GAUGE

SWEATER

22 stitches and 30 rows to 14" (10cm) using size 6 (4mm) needles and DK weight yarn, measured over stockinette stitch.

PANTS

22 stitches and 30 rows to 4" (10cm) using size 6 (4mm) needles and DK weight yarn, measured over stockinette stitch.

HAT/RAIN BOOTS

22 stitches and 30 rows to 4" (10cm) using size 6 (4mm) needles and DK weight yarn, measured over stockinette stitch.

ABBREVIATION

C6B Cable 6 back: Slip the next 3 stitches onto a cable needle and hold these at the back of the work, knit 3 from the left-hand needle, and then knit the 3 stitches from the cable needle.

PANTS

Front

Leg (make 2)

Using size 3 (3.25mm) needles and B, cast on 19 stitches.

Row 1: K1, (p1, k1) to end.
Row 2: P1, (k1, p1) to end.
Repeat rows 1 and 2 once more.
Row 5: K2, m1, (k5, m1) to last 2 stitches, k2—23 stitches.

Row 6: Purl.
Row 7: Knit.
Row 8: Purl.
Repeat rows 7 and 8 8 more times, ending with a wrong-side row.
Do not bind off. Leave the stitches on a holder.

Join the 2 legs of the front as follows:
With right-sides facing, knit across 22 stitches of the left leg, knit the last stitch of the left leg together with the first stitch of the right leg, knit to end—45 stitches.
Row 2: Purl.
Row 3: K4, k2tog, (k3, k2tog) to last 4 stitches, k4—37 stitches.
Row 4: Purl.
Row 5: Knit.
Repeat rows 4 and 5 9 more times, ending with right-side row.
Row 24 (WS): Knit (this creates a ridge for the turn-over hem at the top of the pants.)
Row 25: Knit.
Row 26: Purl.
Row 27: Knit.
Bind off.

Back

Work the same as for the Front of the pants.

Suspenders (make 2)

Using size 3 (3.25mm) needles and B, cast on

5 stitches.
Row 1: Knit.
Row 2: K1, p3, k1.
Repeat rows 1 and 2 until the piece measures 12⅛" (31cm) from cast-on edge, ending with a wrong-side row.
Bind off.

SWEATER

Back

Using size 3 (3.25mm) needles and A, cast on 38 stitches.
Row 1: K2, (p2, k2) to end.
Row 2: P2, (k2, p2) to end.
Row 3: As row 1.
Row 4: Work in rib pattern for 1 stitch, m1, (work in rib pattern for 5 stitches, m1) 7 times, work in rib pattern for 2 stitches—46 stitches.
Repeat row 4 3 more times, ending with a wrong-side row.
Change to size 6 (4mm) needles.
Row 8: *K1, (p1, k1) 3 times, k6, repeat from * twice more, k1, (p1, k1) to end.
Row 9: K1, (p1, k1) 3 times, *p6, k1, (p1, k1) 3 times, repeat from * to end.
Row 10: K1, (p1, k1) 3 times, *k6, k1, (p1, k1) 3 times, repeat from * to end.
Row 11: Work as for row 9.
Row 12: K1, (p1, k1) 3 times, *C6B, k1, (p1, k1) 3 times, repeat from * to end.
Row 13: Work as for row 9.

Row 14: Work as for row 10.
Row 15: Work as for row 9.
Row 16: Work as for row 10.
Row 17: Work as for row 9.
Row 18: Work as for row 10.**
Repeat rows 9 through 14 5 more times, then repeat rows 9 through 12 once more.
Next row: Work as row 9.
Next row: Work in pattern for 9 stitches, bind off center 28 stitches, work in pattern for 9 stitches.
Do not bind off. Leave both sets of shoulder stitches on holders.

Front
Work as for back until **.
Repeat rows 9 through 14 4 more times.
Row 40: Work as for row 9.
Row 41: Work in pattern for 17 stitches, turn, and keeping pattern correct, work on these 17 stitches only as follows:
Row 42: Work in pattern to end.
Row 43: Work in pattern to last 2 stitches, k2tog.
Row 44: P2tog, work in pattern to end.
Repeat rows 43 and 44 3 more times, ending with a wrong-side row.
Do not bind off. Leave the shoulder stitches on a holder.
Rejoin yarn to remaining stitches, bind off center 12 stitches and work in pattern to end. Work on these 17 stitches as follows:
Row 42: Work in pattern to end.
Row 43: K2tog, work in pattern to end.
Row 44: Work in pattern to last 2 stitches, p2tog.
Repeat rows 43 and 44 3 more times, ending with a wrong-side row.
Do not bind off. Leave the shoulder stitches on a holder.

Neckband
Join the right shoulder using the three-needle

bind-off technique as described on page 26. With right side facing, using size 3 (3.25mm) needles and A, pick up and knit 10 stitches down the left front of the neck, 12 stitches across the center front, 10 stitches up the right front of the neck, and 30 stitches across the back—62 stitches.
Row 1: K2, (p2, k2) to end.
Row 2: P2, (k2, p2) to end.
Row 3: K2, (p2, k2) to end.
Bind off in rib.

SLEEVES (MAKE 2)
Using size 3 (3.25mm) needles and A, cast on 26 stitches.
Row 1: K2, (p2, k2) to end.
Row 2: P2, (k2, p2) to end.
Repeat rows 1 and 2 once more, ending with a wrong-side row.
Change to size 6 (4mm) needles.
Row 5: (K1, p1) to end.
Row 6: (P1, k1) to end.
Repeat rows 5 and 6 12 more times, ending with a wrong-side row.
Bind off in seed stitch.

RAIN BOOTS
Boot (make 2)
Using size 6 (4mm) needles and C, cast on 25 stitches.
Row 1: Knit.
Repeat this row 3 more times.
Row 5: Knit.
Row 6: Purl.
Repeat rows 5 and 6 4 more times, ending with a wrong-side row.
Row 15: K12, m1, k1, m1, k12—27 stitches.
Row 16: P13, m1, p1, m1, p13—29 stitches.
Row 17: K14, m1, k1, m1, k14—31 stitches.
Row 18: P15, m1, p1, m1, p15—33 stitches.
Row 19: K16, m1, k1, m1, k16—35 stitches.
Row 20: Purl.

Row 21: Knit.
Row 22: Purl.
Row 23: Knit.
Row 24: Purl.
Bind off.

Sole (make 2)
Using size 6 (4mm) needles and C, cast on 4 stitches.
Row 1: Knit.
Row 2: K1, (m1, k1) to end—7 stitches.
Row 3: Knit.
Row 4: K1, m1, knit to last stitch, m1, k1—9 stitches.
Row 5: Knit.
Row 6: K1, m1, knit to last stitch, m1, k1—11 stitches.
Row 7: Knit.
Repeat row 7 7 more times
Next row: K1, k2tog, knit to last 3 stitches, k2tog, k1—9 stitches.
Next row: Knit.
Next row: K1, k2tog, knit to last 3 stitches, k2tog, k1—7 stitches.
Next row: Knit.
Next row: K1, k2tog, k1, k2tog, k1—5 stitches.
Bind off, decreasing 1 stitch at each end of bound-off row.

HAT

Using size 6 (4mm) needles and C, cast on 41 stitches.

Row 1 (WS): Purl.
Row 2: K2, k2tog, (k3, k2tog) to last 2 stitches, k2—33 stitches.
Row 3: Purl.
Row 4: Knit.
Row 5: Purl.
Row 6: K1, (k2tog, k2) to end—25 stitches.
Row 7: Purl.
Row 8: Knit.
Row 9: Purl.
Repeat rows 6 through 9 once more—19 stitches.
Next row: K1, (k2tog, k1) to end—13 stitches.
Next row: Purl.
Next row: K1, (k2tog, k1) to end—9 stitches.

Do not bind off. Thread the yarn through the remaining stitches and pull together.

Brim

With right side facing, using size 6 (4mm) needles and C, pick up and knit 40 stitches along the cast-on edge of the hat.
Row 1: Knit.
Repeat row 1 twice more.
Row 4: K5, (m1, k5) to end—47 stitches.
Row 5: Knit.
Repeat row 5 twice more.
Row 8: (K6, m1) to last 5 stitches, k5—54 stitches.
Row 9: Knit.
Bind off.

FISH

Using size 3 (3.25mm) needles and D, cast on 3 stitches.
Row 1: K1, p1, k1.
Row 2: K1, m1, k1, m1, k1—5 stitches.
Row 3: K1, p3, k1.
Row 4: K2, m1, k1, m1, k2—7 stitches.
Row 5: K1, p5, k1.
Row 6: K3, m1, k1, m1, k3—9 stitches.
Row 7: K1, p7, k1.
Row 8: K4, m1, k1, m1, k4—11 stitches.
Row 9: K1, p9, k1.
Row 10: K4, sl2, k1, p2sso, k4—9 stitches.
Row 11: K1, p7, k1
Row 12: K3, sl2, k1, p2sso, k5—7 stitches.
Row 13: K1, p5, k1.
Row 14: K2, sl2, k1, p2sso, k2—5 stitches.
Row 15: K1, p3, k1.
Row 16: K1, sl2, k1, p2sso, k1—3 stitches.
Row 17: K1, p1, k1.
Row 18: K1, m1, k1, m1, k1—5 stitches.
Row 19: K1, p3, k1.
Row 20: K1, (m1, k1) to end—9 stitches.
Bind off.

FINISHING
PANTS

Both the front and back sections of the pants have a hem at the top. Fold the hem inwards along the garter stitch ridge and whip stitch into place.

Join the front and back sections of the pants as follows: Sew the outer seams. Start at top (bound-off edge) and work down to the bottom (cast-on edge). Join the inner leg seams. Starting at the cast-on edge of the right leg, work up to the top, then work down the corresponding seam of the left leg.

Suspenders

At the cast-on edge of each suspender, sew one half of each snap to the wrong side. Sew each suspender in place. Place 4 markers (to indicate where the suspenders are to be attached to the top of the pants) as follows: On the front of the pants, measure 2" (5cm) in from the right side seam and place a marker. Measure 2" (5cm) in from the left side seam and place a marker. Repeat this on the back of the pants.
Sew the remaining half of each snap to the outside of the front of the pants as indicated by the 2 markers on this section.
Stitch the suspenders neatly and securely inside the top of the back section of the pants as follows:
Sew the bound-off edge of one of the suspenders to the position of the right back marker, then sew the bound-off edge of the other suspender to the position of the left back marker.
Now cross the suspenders so that the left back strap fastens to the right front stud button and vice versa.
Sew the 2 buttons to the right side of each cast-on edge of the straps.

SWEATER

Join the left shoulder seam using the three-needle bind-off technique as described on page 26.

Sleeves

Fold sleeve in half lengthwise and mark the center of the bound-off edge with a stitch marker. Line this marker up with the shoulder seam and tack the sleeve in place. Then sew the sleeve to the body. Attach both sleeves in the same way.
Join both side and sleeve seams.

HAT

Sew together the seam of the hat by working from the edge of the brim all the way to the top of the hat.

RAIN BOOTS

Fold the boot in half lengthwise and, starting at the cast-on edge, sew the 2 side edges together, forming a seam which runs down the back of the boot. Then attach the sole by sewing around the edges of the sole, joining it to the bound-off edge of the boot.

FISHING ROD

Using the photograph as a guide, make the fishing rod as follows: Cut a length of black sewing thread, approximately 10" (25cm). Starting about a quarter of the way along the wooden dowelling, stretch the thread so that it is parallel with the dowelling, ensuring that you have a good 3" (7.5cm) hanging free at the end, then secure by wrapping craft wire around the dowelling in three places, making sure the third is at the very tip of the rod. Sew the fish to the end of the thread.

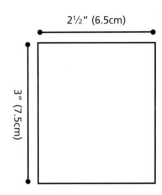

2½" (6.5cm)

3" (7.5cm)

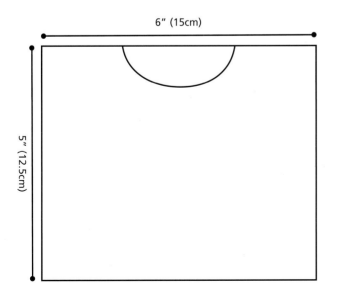

6" (15cm)

5" (12.5cm)

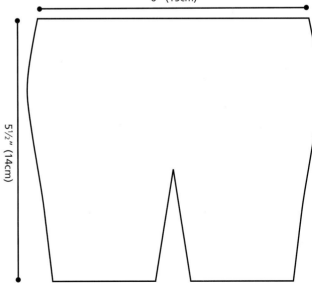

6" (15cm)

5½" (14cm)

Graduation Bear

Celebrate the end of high school or college with Graduation Bear. The cap and gown, which can be knit in any school color, make this bear the perfect gift for a graduating student.

SKILL LEVEL
Simple

MATERIALS
For the gown
- 112 yds (104m) sport weight yarn (2) fine (A). The bear's outfit opposite uses 2 balls Rowan Classic Bamboo Soft, 100% bamboo, 1 oz (50g), 112 yds (102m), 115 Black

For the cap
- 126 yds (102m) sport weight yarn (2) fine (B). The bear's outfit opposite uses 1 ball Rowan Cotton Glace, 100% cotton, 1 oz (50g), 137 yds (115m), 727 Black
- Sizes 3 and 5 (3.25mm and 3.75mm) needles (or size needed to obtain gauge)
- Cardboard, 3½ x 3½" (9x9cm)
- 1 7mm snap
- Plain white paper measuring 5 x 3½" (4x9cm)
- ⅛" wide red ribbon approximately 4" (10cm) in length
- Tapestry needle

GAUGE
25 stitches and 30 rows to 4" (10cm) using size 5 (3.75mm) needles and sport weight yarn, measured over stockinette stitch.

GOWN
Using size 5 (3.75mm) needles and A, cast on 45 stitches.
Row 1: Knit.
Row 2: K1, purl to last stitch, k1.
Repeat rows 1 and 2 5 more times, ending

with a wrong-side row.
Row 13: K4, m1, k1, m1, (k6, m1, k1, m1) to last 5 stitches, k5—57 stitches.
Row 14: K1, purl to last stitch, k1.
Row 15: Knit.
Row 16: K1, purl to last stitch, k1.
Row 17: K5, m1, k1, m1, (k8, m1, k1, m1) to last 6 stitches, k6—69 stitches.
Row 18: K1, purl to last stitch, k1.
Row 19: Knit.
Row 20: K1, purl to last stitch, k1.
Row 21: Knit.
Row 22: K1, purl to last stitch, k1.
Row 23: K6, m1, k1, m1, (k10, m1, k1, m1) to last 7 stitches, k7—81 stitches.
Row 24: K1, purl to last stitch, k1.
Row 25: K14, turn and work on these 14 stitches only as follows:
Row 26: K1, purl to last stitch, k1.
Row 27: Knit.
Row 28: K1, purl to last stitch, k1.
Repeat rows 27 and 28 11 more times.
Do not bind off. Leave these stitches on a holder.
With right side facing, rejoin yarn to the remaining stitches, knit 53, and turn. Work on these 53 stitches stitches only as follows:
Row 26: K1, purl to last stitch, k1.
Row 27: Knit.
Row 28: K1, purl to last stitch, k1.
Repeat last 2 rows 11 more times.
Do not bind off. Leave the stitches on a holder.
With right side facing, rejoin yarn to remaining 14 stitches. Work on these 14 stitches only as follows:
Next row: K1, purl to last stitch, k1.

Next row: Knit.
Next row: K1, purl to last stitch, k1.
Repeat last 2 rows 11 more times.
Do not bind off. Leave the stitches on a holder. You will now have 3 sets of stitches on holders. Join these 3 sections as follows:
With right side facing, knit across 14 stitches from the left section, 53 stitches from the middle section, and 14 stitches from the right section—81 stitches.
Next row: K1, purl to last stitch, k1.
Next row: Knit.
Next row: K1, purl to last stitch, k1.
Repeat the last 2 rows until the gown measures 10⅜" (27cm) from cast-on edge.
Bind off.

CAP
Mortar board (make 2)
Using size 3 (3.25mm) needles and B, cast on 23 stitches.
Row 1: Knit.
Row 2: Purl.
Repeat rows 1 and 2 14 more times, ending with a wrong-side row.
Bind off.

Band
Using size 3 (3.25mm) needles and B, cast on 9 stitches.
Row 1: Knit.
Row 2: Purl.
Repeat rows 1 and 2 until work measures 7" (18cm) from cast-on edge, ending with a wrong-side row.
Bind off.

SCROLL

Using the photograph as a guide, roll the paper lengthwise into a scroll and tie the ribbon around the center, securing it with a bow.

FINISHING
GOWN

Sew the snap to the front opening of the gown, approximately 1⅝" (4cm) down from the cast-on edge. When the snap is fastened, the cast-on edges of the gown will curl naturally, creating a collar.

CAP

Sew both mortar-board pieces together, joining 3 side seams and leaving the fourth open. Slip the cardboard inside, and then join the final seam.

Create a circle with the band by sewing the cast-on edge to the bound-off edge. Center the band underneath the mortar board and whip stitch into place.

Tassel

Cut 4 9½" (24cm) lengths of yarn. Fold each length in half and then, with another piece of yarn, tie all 4 together at the looped end. Use this yarn to attach the tassel neatly and securely to the top center of the cap.

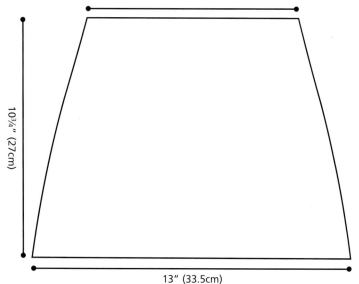

4½" (11.5cm)

10¾" (27cm)

13" (33.5cm)

Aladdin Bear

With his cute bolero and baggy pants, Aladdin Bear is ready to take you on a magic carpet ride. Boys and girls alike will love this bear—find a lamp for him to rub and see if his wish will be granted!

SKILL LEVEL
SIMPLE

MATERIALS
For the pants
- 93 yds (85m) worsted weight yarn 4 medium (A). The bear's outfit on page 60 uses 1 ball Rowan Handknit Cotton, 100% cotton, 1 oz (50g), 93 yds (85m), 263 Bleached

For the bolero
- 93 yds (85m) worsted weight yarn 4 medium (B). The bear's outfit on page 60 uses 1 ball Rowan Handknit Cotton, 314 Decadent
- Sizes 3 and 6 (3.25mm and 4mm) needles (or size needed to obtain gauge)
- 14" (35cm) of gold ribbon, approximately 1" (2.5cm) wide
- Small piece of sticky backed hook-and-eye tape.
- Tapestry needle

GAUGE
20 stitches and 28 rows to 4" (10cm) using size 6 (4mm) needles and worsted weight yarn, measured over stockinette stitch.

PANTS
Front
Leg (make 2)
Using size 3 (3.25mm) needles and A, cast on 17 stitches.
Row 1: K1, (p1, k1) to end.
Row 2: P1, (k1, p1) to end.
Repeat rows 1 and 2 once more.
Change to size 6 (4mm) needles.

Row 5: K1, m1, (k5, m1) 3 times, k1— 21 stitches.
Row 6: Purl.
Row 7: Knit.
Row 8: Purl.
Repeat rows 7 and 8 6 more times.
Do not bind off. Leave these stitches on a holder.
Join the 2 legs of the front as follows: With right sides facing and using size 3 (3.25mm) needles, knit across 20 stitches of left leg, knit the last stitch of the left leg together with the first stitch of the right leg, knit to end— 41 stitches.
Next row: Purl.
Next row: K5, k2tog, (k3, k2tog) to last 4 stitches, k4—34 stitches.
Next row: Purl.
Next row: Knit.
Next row: Purl.
Repeat the last 2 rows 7 more times, ending with a wrong-side row.
Next row: (K1, p1) to end.
Repeat last row 3 more times, ending with a wrong-side row.
Bind off in rib pattern.

Back
Work as for the Front.

BOLERO (KNITTED ALL IN ONE PIECE)
Using size 6 (4mm) needles and B, cast on 27 stitches.
Row 1: Knit.
Row 2: K1, p25, k1.
Repeat rows 1 and 2 7 more times, ending with a wrong-side row.

Row 17: K8, turn and work on these 8 stitches only as follows:
Row 18: K1, p6, k1.
Row 19: Knit.
Row 20: K1, p6, k1.
Repeat rows 19 and 20 7 more times, ending with a wrong-side row.
Row 35: Knit to last 3 stitches, k2tog, k1— 7 stitches.
Row 36: K1, p2tog, purl to last stitch, k1— 6 stitches.
Repeat rows 35 and 36 once more—4 stitches.
Row 39: K1, k2tog, k1—3 stitches.
Row 40: K1, p1, k1.
Bind off.

With right side facing, rejoin yarn to remaining stitches, bind off center 11 stitches and knit to end. Continue as follows:
Row 18: K1, p6, k1.
Row 19: Knit.
Row 20: K1, p6, k1.
Repeat rows 19 and 20 7 more times, ending with a wrong-side row.

Row 35: K1, k2togtbl, knit to end—7 stitches.
Row 36: K1, purl to last 3 stitches, p2togtbl, k1—6 stitches.
Repeat rows 35 and 36 once more—4 stitches.
Row 39: K1, k2togtbl, k1—3 stitches.
Row 40: K1, p1, k1.
Bind off.

FINISHING
PANTS
Join the front and back of the pants as follows: Sew the outer side seams. Start at the top (bound-off edge) and work down to the bottom (cast-on edge). Then join the inner leg seams. Starting at the cast-on edge of the right leg, work up to the top, and then work down the corresponding seam of the left leg.

BOLERO
Fold over the 2 narrow strips so that they become the 2 fronts of the bolero. Stitch into place by joining the bound-off edge of the right front to the base of the right side seam, and then the bound-off edge of the left front to the base of the left side seam.

WAISTBAND
Fix the ribbon around the waistband of the pants and use hook-and-eye tape to fasten.

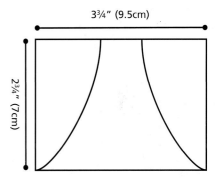

3¾" (9.5cm)

2¾" (7cm)

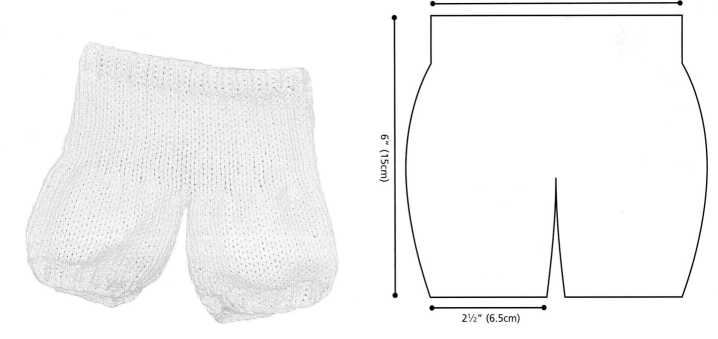

5½" (14cm)

6" (15cm)

2½" (6.5cm)

Complex Medium-Sized Bear

This complex bear is perfect for more advanced knitters. With more sophisticated shaping and a two-tone option, this bear is perfect as a collectible or for the kids to play with.

FINISHED SIZE

Height: 10⅝" (27cm)
Diameter (around body): 8" (20.5cm)

MATERIALS

Option A (Beige)

- 153 yds (140m) worsted weight yarn **4** medium (A). The bear on page 70 uses 1 ball Rowan Kid Classic, 70% lambswool, 26% kid mohair, 4% nylon, 1 oz (50g), 153 yds (140m), 857 Oats
- 123 yds (113m) DK weight yarn **3** light (B). The bear on page 70 uses 1 ball Rowan Wool Cotton, 50% wool, 50% cotton, 1 oz (50g), 123 yds (113m), 900 Antique

Option B (Cream)

- 153 yds (140m) worsted weight yarn **4** medium (A). The bear on page 66 uses 1 ball Rowan Kid Classic, 828 Feather
- 123 yds (113m) DK weight yarn **3** light (B). The bear on page 66 uses 1 ball Rowan Wool Cotton, 50% wool, 50% cotton, 1 oz (50g), 123 yds (113m), 929 Dream
- 175 yds (160m) sport weight yarn **2** fine for facial features. The bear on page 66 uses small amount Rowan Calmer, 75% cotton, 25% acrylic, 1 oz (50g), 175 yds (160m), 481 Coffee Bean
- Size 5 (3.75mm) needles (or size needed to obtain gauge)
- Tapestry needle
- 1¾ oz (50g) toy stuffing

GAUGE

25 stitches and 32 rows to 4" (10cm) using size 5 (3.75mm) needles and worsted weight yarn, measured over stockinette stitch.

BODY

Sides (make 2)

Using A, cast on 9 stitches.
Row 1 (RS): Purl.
Row 2: Knit.
Row 3: P4, m1, p1, m1, p4—11 stitches.
Keeping shaping as set (increasing either side of center stitch), repeat rows 2 and 3 until there are 21 stitches, ending with a right-side row.
Row 14: Knit.
Row 15: Purl.
Row 16: Knit.
Row 17: P10, m1, p1, m1, p10—23 stitches.
Row 18: Knit.
Row 19: Purl. *
Repeat rows 18 and 19 11 more times, ending with a right-side row.
Row 42: Knit.
Row 43: P9, p2tog, p1, p2togtbl, purl to end—21 stitches.
Row 44: Knit.
Row 45: P8, p2tog, p1, p2togtbl, purl to end—19 stitches.
Row 46: K7, k2togtbl, k1, k2tog, knit to end—17 stitches.
Row 47: P6, p2tog, p1, p2togtbl, purl to end—15 stitches.
Row 48: K5, k2togtbl, k1, k2tog, knit to end—13 stitches.
Row 49: P4, p2tog, p1, p2togtbl, purl to end—11 stitches.
Row 50: K3, k2togtbl, k1, k2tog, knit to end—9 stitches.
Row 51: (P2tog) 4 times, p1—5 stitches.
Do not bind off. Thread yarn through the remaining stitches and pull together to secure.

HEAD

Left side

Using A, cast on 13 stitches.
Row 1: Purl.
Row 2: Knit.
Repeat rows 1 and 2 once more.
Row 5: P1, m1, purl to last stitch, m1, p1—15 stitches.
Row 6: Knit.
Repeat last 2 rows once more—17 stitches.
Row 9: Using A p15, using B k1, m1, k1—18 stitches.
Row 10: Using B p1, m1, p2, using A knit to end—19 stitches.
Row 11: Using A p15, using B k3, m1, k1—20 stitches.
Row 12: Using B p1, m1, p2, using A knit to end—21 stitches.
Row 13: Using A, p15, using B k5, m1, k1—22 stitches.
Row 14: Using B p8, using A k14.
Row 15: Using A p13, using B k9.
Row 16: Using B p10, using A k12.
Row 17: Using A p12, using B k10.
Row 18: Using B p10, using A k12.
Row 19: Using A p12, using B k10.
Row 20: Using B, bind off 5 stitches, p5, using A k12—17 stitches.
Row 21: Using A p12, using yarn B k2, k2tog, k1—16 stitches.
Row 22: Keeping A and B as set, bind off 4 stitches, knit to end—12 stitches.
Row 23: Purl.
Row 24: Knit.
Row 25: P1, p2tog, purl to last 3 stitches, p2tog, p1—10 stitches.
Row 26: K1, k2tog, knit to last 3 stitches,

k2tog, k1—8 stitches.
Bind off.

Right side
Using A, cast on 13 stitches.
Row 1: Purl.
Row 2: Knit.
Row 3: Purl.
Row 4: K1, m1, knit to last stitch, m1, k1—
15 stitches.
Row 5: Purl.
Repeat rows 4 and 5 once more—17 stitches.
Row 8: Using A k15, using B p1, m1, p1—
18 stitches.
Row 9: Using B k1, m1, k2, using A purl to
end—19 stitches.
Row 10: Using A k15, using B p3, m1, p1—
20 stitches.
Row 11: Using B k1, m1, k4, using A purl to
end—21 stitches.
Row 12: Using A k15, using B p5, m1, p1—
22 stitches.
Row 13: Using B k8, using A p14.
Row 14: Using A k13, using B p9.
Row 15: Using B k10, using A p12.
Row 16: Using A k12, using B p10.
Row 17: Using B k10, using A p12.
Row 18: Using A k12, using B p10.
Row 19: Using B bind off 5 stitches, k5,
using A p12—17 stitches.
Row 20: Using A k12, using B p2, p2tog, p1—
16 stitches.
Row 21: Keeping yarns A and B as set, bind
off 4 stitches, purl to end—12 stitches.
Row 22: Knit.
Row 23: Purl.
Row 24: K1, k2tog, knit to last 3 stitches,
k2tog, k1—10 stitches.
Row 25: P1, p2tog, purl to last 3 stitches,
p2tog, p1—8 stitches.
Bind off.

Head gusset
Using A, cast on 4 stitches.
Row 1: Purl.
Row 2: Knit.
Row 3: P1 (m1, k1) to end—7 stitches.
Row 4: Knit.
Row 5: P1, m1, purl to last stitch, m1, p1—
9 stitches.
Repeat rows 4 and 5 twice more—13 stitches.
Row 10: Knit.
Row 11: Purl.
Row 12: Knit.
Row 13: P1, m1, purl to last stitch, m1, p1—
15 stitches.
Row 14: Knit.
Row 15: Purl.
Row 16: Knit.
Row 17: Purl.
Row 18: Knit.
Row 19: P1, m1, purl to last stitch, m1, p1—
17 stitches.
Row 20: Knit.
Row 21: Purl.
Row 22: Knit.
Row 23: Purl.
Row 24: Knit.
Row 25: P2tog, purl to last 2 stitches, p2tog—
15 stitches.
Row 26: Knit.
Row 27: P2tog, purl to last 2 stitches, p2tog—
13 stitches.
Repeat rows 26 and 27 until 9 stitches remain.
Row 32: Knit.
Row 33: Purl.
Repeat rows 32 and 33 twice more.
Row 38: Knit.
Change to yarn B and continue as follows:
Row 39: Knit.
Row 40: Purl.
Row 41: Knit.
Repeat rows 40 and 41 once more.

Row 44: P2tog, purl to last 2 stitches, p2tog—
7 stitches.
Row 45: Knit.
Repeat rows 44 and 45 twice more.
Row 50: Sl2, p1, p2sso.
Fasten off.

LEGS (MAKE 2)
Using A, cast on 17 stitches.
Row 1: Purl.
Row 2: Knit.
Row 3: P1, m1, purl to last stitch, m1, p1—
19 stitches.
Repeat rows 2 and 3 once more—21 stitches.
Row 6: Knit.
Row 7: Purl.
Row 8: Knit.
Repeat rows 7 and 8 6 more times.
Row 21: P8, p2tog, p1, p2togtbl, p8—19
stitches.
Row 22: Knit.
Row 23: Purl.
Row 24: Knit.
Row 25: P9, m1, p1, m1, p9—21 stitches.
Row 26: K10, m1, k1, m1, k10—23 stitches.
Keeping shaping as set (increasing either side
of center stitch), repeat rows 25 and 26 until
there are 31 stitches, ending with a wrong-side
row.
Next row: Purl.
Next row: Knit.
Next row: Purl.
Bind off.

FEET PADS (MAKE 2)

Using B, cast on 3 stitches.

Row 1: Purl.

Row 2: K1, m1, k1, m1, k1—5 stitches.

Row 3: Purl.

Row 4: K1, m1, knit to last stitch, m1, k1—7 stitches.

Repeat rows 3 and 4 once more—9 stitches.

Row 7: Purl.

Row 8: Knit.

Row 9: Purl.

Repeat rows 8 and 9 twice more.

Row 14: K2, k2tog, k1, k2tog, k2—7 stitches.

Row 15: Purl.

Row 16: K1, k2tog, k1, k2tog, k1—5 stitches.

Bind off and, **at the same time**, k2tog at each end of the bind-off row.

ARMS

Inner arms (make 2)

Using B, cast on 3 stitches.

Row 1: Purl.

Row 2: K1, m1, k1, m1, k1—5 stitches.

Row 3: Purl.

Row 4: K1, m1, k3, m1, k1—7 stitches.

Row 5: Purl.

Row 6: K1, m1, k5, m1, k1—9 stitches.

Row 7: Purl.

Row 8: Knit.

Row 9: Purl.

Change yarn to A and continue as follows:

Row 10: Knit.

Row 11: Knit.

Row 12: Purl.

Repeat last 2 rows 11 more times.

Next row: Knit.

Next row: P1, p2tog, p3, p2togtbl, p1—7 stitches.

Next row: Knit.

Next row: P1, p2tog, p1, p2togtbl, p1—5 stitches.

Do not bind off. Thread yarn through the remaining stitches and pull together to secure.

Outer arms (make 2)

Using A, cast on 3 stitches.

Row 1: Knit.

Row 2: P1, m1, p1, m1, p1—5 stitches.

Row 3: Knit.

Row 4: P1, m1, p3, m1, p1—7 stitches.

Row 5: Knit.

Row 6: P1, m1, p5, m1, p1—9 stitches.

Row 7: Knit.

Row 8: Purl.

Repeat rows 7 and 8 13 more times.

Next row: Knit.

Next row: P1, p2tog, p3, p2togtbl, p1—7 stitches.

Next row: Knit.

Next row: P1, p2tog, p1, p2togtbl, p1—5 stitches.

Do not bind off. Thread yarn through the remaining stitches and pull together to secure.

EARS (MAKE 2)

Cast on 7 stitches.

Row 1: Knit.

Row 2: Purl.

Repeat rows 1 and 2 once more.

Row 5: K2tog, knit to last 2 stitches, k2tog—5 stitches.

Bind off and, **at the same time**, k2tog at each end of the bind-off row. Leave a long enough tail to shape the ear and attach it to the head.

FINISHING

HEAD

Using A and starting at the cast-on edges, sew together the gusset and left side of head until you reach the beginning of the snout. Change to yarn B and continue sewing the seam until you reach the tip of snout. Attach the right side of the head in the same way.

Using B and starting at the tip of the snout, sew the front seam of the 2 sides until you reach the end of the snout. Change to yarn A and continue sewing the seam until you are 2/3 of the way along the 2 cast-on edges of the sides. Using the opening that you have left, stuff the head until it is firm (using the photograph as a guide to help you to achieve a good shape). Finally, weave A around the side of the opening and pull, gathering the seams together (like a drawstring). Fasten securely.

FACIAL FEATURES

Using the brown yarn (Rowan Calmer shade 481), sew the bear's facial features as follows:

Eyes

Measure approximately 1¾" (4.5cm) up each gusset seam from the tip of the snout. *Use a long sewing needle to create each eye as follows: Leaving a long tail for securing, insert the needle just to the right of the gusset seam and then bring it out to just to the left of the gusset seam. Take the yarn back through once more in the same way. Then insert the needle into the original hole and, this time, take it down through the center of the head and out through the underside. Now return to the long thread that you left at the beginning and thread this onto your needle. Insert it into the hole to the left of the gusset and take it down through the center of the head and out through the under-side. Pulling gently on these 2 yarns will set the eyes further into the bear's head, giving your bear's face character. When you have sewn both eyes, pull gently on these yarns to create a face you are happy with. Then secure the yarns firmly so as to keep the features you have created.

Nose and mouth

The nose is an upside-down triangle. Use the gusset seams where they taper to a point for the snout as a guide as to where you need to sew to get a good shape. Insert the needle into the left gusset seam and take it horizontally under the knitting and out through the right gusset seam. Now Insert it into the left seam again but, this time, just below where you originally went in. Again, take it horizontally under the knitting and out of the right seam, just below the previous stitch. Continue in this way, shortening each consecutive stitch, until the nose tapers to a point at the tip of the snout. Next, starting at the tip of the snout, sew a long single stitch roughly 5⁄8" (1.5cm) down and insert the needle into the head, then bring it out 1⁄4" (0.75cm) to the left and slightly lower. Create a diagonal single stitch by inserting the needle back in through the base of the 5⁄8" (1.5cm) vertical stitch. Then, bring the needle back out approximately 1⁄4" (0.75cm) to the right and slightly lower (opposite to last time) and create a second diagonal stitch by inserting the needle back in through the base of the 5⁄8" (1.5cm) vertical stitch. Take the needle down through the center of the head and out through the underside. Fasten securely.

BODY

Sew the 2 pieces together as follows (the seams are at the center front and center back of the body): Starting at the cast-on edge, sew the first seam all the way to the top of the body. Sew the other seam in the same way, but stop approximately 2⁄3 of the way up. Join the cast-on edges of the 2 pieces. Using the opening that you have left, stuff the body until it is firm and roughly 7¾" (20cm) in diameter (using the photograph as a guide to help you to achieve a good shape). Sew up the remaining 1⁄3 of the second seam. Fasten securely.

ARMS

Each arm has an outer section and inner section. The inner section has a paw pad in the contrasting yarn. Join the inner section to the outer section starting at the top of the arm, working down one side and then up the other, stopping approximately 2⁄3 of the way up. Then, using the opening you have left, stuff the arm until it is firm, then sew up the remaining 1⁄3 of the seam. Fasten securely.

LEGS

Each leg has been knitted in 1 piece, and will have a foot pad attached at the sole. Fold the leg in half lengthwise and sew the 2 side edges together, forming a seam which runs down the back of the leg. When folding the leg in half, you will have folded the cast-on edge in half, too—join these 2 edges together, creating a seam that runs across the top of the leg from front to back.

Using the opening that you have at the base of the foot, stuff the leg until it is firm (using the photograph as a guide to help you to achieve a good shape) and then attach the foot pad by sewing around the edges of the pad, joining it to the bound-off edge of the leg.

EARS

Mark the position of the ears as follows: Measure approximately 2" (5cm) from the beginning of the color change of the snout, up the head seam. *Place the ear across the seam and attach as follows: Using the long tail that you left when binding off, give the ear some shape by sewing the tail around the outer edge of the ear, and then use the same thread to attach to the head.

ASSEMBLING THE BEAR

Sew the head securely to the top center of the body. Stitch the arms to the body at the beginning of the shoulder shaping. Sew the legs to the body approximately 3⁄8" (1cm) from the beginning of the side shaping.

Safari Bear

Join Safari Bear on the lookout for wild animals! With his butterfly net and khaki safari suit, he's definitely ready for adventure.

SKILL LEVEL
Simple

MATERIALS
For the shirt and shorts
- 93 yds (85m) worsted weight yarn (4) medium (A). The bear's outfit opposite uses 1 ball Rowan Handknit Cotton, 100% cotton, 1 oz (50g), 93 yds (85m), 205 Line

For the butterfly
- 126 yds (115m) worsted weight yarn (4) fine (B). The bear's outfit opposite uses 1 ball Rowan Cotton Glace, 100% cotton, 1 oz (50g), 137 yds (115m), 832 Persimmon
- Sizes 2, 3, and 6 (3mm, 3.25mm, and 4mm) needles (or size needed to obtain gauge)
- 6 5mm buttons, such as Rowan 00333
- 3 7mm snaps
- 6" (15cm) length of 28 gauge craft wire
- Craft glue
- 2 3mm black beads, such as Rowan 01017
- 5" (12.5cm) length of doweling
- Small piece of netting fabric
- Small amount of white yarn
- Tapestry needle

GAUGE
20 stitches and 28 rows to 4" (10cm) using size 6 (4mm) needles and worsted weight yarn, measured over stockinette stitch.

SHORTS
Front
Leg (make 2)
Using size 6 (4mm) needles and A, cast on 17 stitches.
Row 1: Knit.

Row 2: Purl.
Row 3: Purl (this creates a ridge for the hem and reverses the stockinette stitch.)
Row 4: Knit.
Row 5: Purl.
Repeat rows 4 and 5 5 more times.
Do not bind off. Leave the stitches on a holder.
Join the 2 legs of the front as follows: With right sides facing, knit across 16 stitches of the left leg, knit the last stitch of the left leg together with the first stitch of the right leg, knit to end—33 stitches.
Row 2: Purl.
Row 3: K2, k2tog, (k1, k2tog) to last 2 stiches, k2—23 stitches.
Row 4: Purl.
Row 5: Knit.
Row 6: Purl.
Repeat rows 5 and 6 5 more times, ending with a wrong-side row.
Row 17: K3, (k2tog, k3) to end—19 stitches.
Row 18: Purl.
Bind off.

Back
Work as for the Front.

SHIRT
Back
Using size 6 (4mm) needles and A, cast on 25 stitches.
Row 1: Knit.
Row 2: Purl.
Repeat rows 1 and 2 14 more times, ending with a wrong-side row.
Next row: K7, bind off center 11 stitches, k7.
Do not bind off. Leave the 2 sets of shoulder stitches on a holder.

Right front
Using size 6 (4mm) needles and A, cast on 14 stitches.
Row 1: Knit.
Row 2: P13, k1.
Repeat rows 1 and 2 10 more times, ending with a wrong-side row.
Row 23: Bind off 4 stitches, knit to end—10 stitches.
Row 24: Purl.
Row 25: K1, k2togtbl, knit to end—9 stitches.
Repeat rows 24 and 25 twice more—7 stitches.
Row 30: Purl.
Row 31: Knit.
Do not bind off. Leave the shoulder stitches on a holder.

Left front
Using size 6 (4mm) needles and A, cast on 14 stitches.
Row 1: Knit.
Row 2: K1, p13.
Repeat rows 1 and 2 9 more times, ending with a wrong-side row.
Row 21: Knit.
Row 22: Bind off 4 stitches, purl to end—10 stitches.
Row 23: Knit.
Row 24: K1, p2tog, purl to end—9 stitches.
Repeat rows 23 and 24 twice more—7 stitches.
Row 29: Knit.
Row 30: Purl.
Row 31: Knit.
Do not bind off. Leave the shoulder stitches on a holder.

Join both shoulder seams using the three-needle bind-off technique as described on page 26, then work the collar as follows: Using size 3 (3.25mm) needles and A, and with the wrong side facing, pick up and knit 13 stitches up the left of the neck, 15 stitches across the back, and 13 stitches down the right of the neck—41 stitches.
Row 1: Purl.
Row 2: Knit.
Row 3: Purl.
Repeat rows 2 and 3 once more.
Bind off.

Sleeves

Using size 6 (4mm) needles and A, cast on 20 stitches.
Row 1: Knit.

Row 2: Purl.
Row 3: Purl (this creates a ridge for the hem and reverses the stockinette stitch).
Row 4: Knit.
Row 5: Purl.
Repeat rows 4 and 5 5 more times, ending with a wrong-side row.
Bind off.

Shirt Pockets

Using size 3 (3.25mm) needles and A, cast on 7 stitches.
Row 1: Knit.
Row 2: K1, p5, k1.
Repeat rows 1 and 2 3 more times, ending with a wrong-side row.
Bind off.

Short Pockets

Using size 3 (3.25mm) needles and A, cast on 9 stitches.
Row 1: Knit.
Row 2: K1, p7, k1.
Repeat rows 1 and 2 4 more times, ending with a wrong-side row.
Bind off.

BUTTERFLY

Using size 2 (3mm) needles and B, cast on 9 stitches.
Row 1: Knit.
Row 2: Purl.
Row 3: K2tog, k5, k2tog—7 stitches.
Row 4: P2tog, p3, p2tog—5 stitches.
Row 5: K2tog, k1, k2tog—3 stitches.
Row 6: Purl.
Row 7: K1, m1, knit to last stitch, m1 , k1—5 stitches.
Row 8: P1, m1, purl to last stitch, m1 , p1—7 stitches.
Row 9: K1, m1, knit to last stitch, m1, k1—9 stitches.
Row 10: Purl.
Row 11: Knit.
Bind off.

FINISHING
SHORTS

Both the front and back sections of the shorts have a hem at the bottom of each leg. Fold the hem outwards along the ridge and whip stitch into place on the right side of the shorts.
Join both front and back sections of the shorts as follows: Sew the outer seams. Start at the top (bound-off edge) and work down to the bottom (cast-on edge). Now join the inner leg seams. Starting at the cast-on edge of the right leg, work up to the top, and then work down the corresponding seam of the left leg.

Using the photograph as a guide, sew one button on each pocket. Sew pockets onto the shorts as in the photograph, positioning pockets over the side seams.

SHIRT
Sleeves
Both sleeves have a hem at the cast-on edge. Fold the hem outwards along the ridge and slip stitch into place on the right side of each sleeve.

Fold sleeve in half lengthwise and mark the center of the bound-off edge with a stitch marker. Line this marker up with the shoulder seam and tack the sleeve in place. Now sew the sleeve to the body. Attach both sleeves in the same way.
Join both side and sleeve seams.

Using the photograph as a guide, sew buttons into place as follows: 1 on each pocket and 1 on each turn-back on the sleeves. Sew pockets onto the fronts, as in the photograph. Sew snaps to the front opening, positioning 1 just below the neck, 1 just above the cast on edge, and the other in between.

BUTTERFLY
Cut a length of craft wire, twist it around the center of the butterfly (the narrowest point), and bend the 2 ends so that they create the antennae. Attach a black bead to the top of each antenna.

BUTTERFLY NET
From the net fabric, cut a triangle approximately 5½" (14cm) along its base, with the other 2 sides measuring approximately 2½" (7.5cm). Fold the triangle in half and join

the two edges of the lower base edge. Carefully thread wire in and out of the other 2 edges and shape this edge into a circle, twisting the 2 ends of wire together where they meet. Using a small amount of white yarn, apply craft glue to hold the yarn in place, and using the photograph as a guide, wrap the length of yarn around one end of the doweling, securing the net wire in place. Wrap another length of yarn around the other end of the doweling to form the handle.

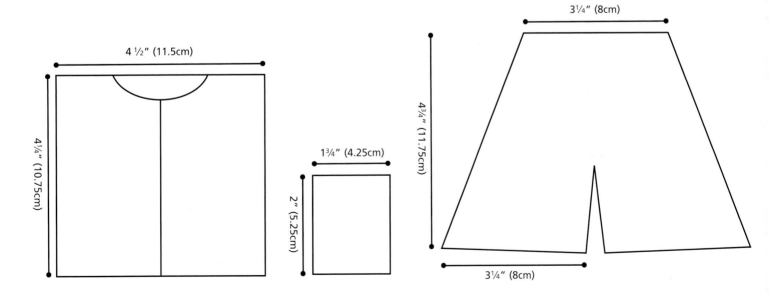

Newborn Baby Bear

This wonderful little bear is the perfect way to celebrate the birth of a new baby. With a beautifully detailed blanket and adorable jacket, Newborn Baby Bear is sure to become a family heirloom.

SKILL LEVEL
Advanced

MATERIALS
For the jacket and blanket
- 246 yds (226m) DK weight yarn (3) light (A). The bear's outfit opposite uses 2 balls Rowan Wool Cotton, 50% wool, 50% cotton, 1 oz (50g), 123 yds (113m), 900 Antique

For the blanket
- 123 yds (113m) DK weight yarn (3) light (B). The bear's outfit opposite uses 1 ball Rowan Wool Cotton, 50% wool, 50% cotton, 1 oz (50g), 123 yds (113m), 951 Tender
- 123 yds (113m) DK weight yarn (3) light (C). The bear's outfit opposite uses 1 ball Rowan Wool Cotton, 50% wool, 50% cotton, 1 oz (50g), 123 yds (113m), 901 Citron
- 123 yds (113m) DK weight yarn (3) light (D). The bear's outfit opposite uses 1 ball Rowan Wool Cotton, 50% wool, 50% cotton, 1 oz (50g), 123 yds (113m), 941 Clear
- 123 yds (113m) DK weight yarn (3) light (E). The bear's outfit opposite uses 1 ball Rowan Wool Cotton, 50% wool, 50% cotton, 1 oz (50g), 123 yds (113m), 952 Hiss
- Size 6 (4mm) needles (or size needed to obtain gauge)
- Tapestry needle

GAUGE
22 stitches and 30 rows to 4" (10cm) using size 6 (4mm) needles and DK weight yarn, measured over stockinette stitch.

JACKET
Back
Using size 6 (4mm) needles and A, cast on 33 stitches.
Row 1: K1, (p1, k1) to end.
Repeat row 1 27 more times, ending with a wrong-side row.
Row 29: Knit.
Repeat row 29 twice more. *
Row 32: P1, (p2tog, p2) to end—25 stitches.
Row 33: Knit.
Row 34: Purl.
Repeat rows 33 and 34 4 more times, ending with a wrong-side row.
Next row: K7, bind off center 11 stitches, k7. Do not bind off. Leave the two sets of shoulder stitches on a holder.

Right front
Using size 6 (4mm) needles and A, cast on 17 stitches.
Work as for Back until *.
Row 32: P1, (p2tog, p2) to end—13 stitches.
Row 33: Knit.
Row 34: P12, k1.
Repeat rows 33 and 34 twice more. **
Row 39: Bind off 3 stitches, knit to end—10 stitches.
Row 40: Purl to last 3 stitches, p2togtbl, k1—9 stitches.
Row 41: K1, k2togtbl, knit to end—8 stitches.
Row 42: Purl to last 3 stitches, p2togtbl, k1—7 stitches.
Row 43: K7.
Do not bind off. Leave the shoulder stitches on a holder.

Left front
Work as for Right Front until **.
Row 39: Knit.
Row 40: Bind off 3 stitches, purl to end—10 stitches.
Row 41: Knit to last 3 stitches, k2tog, k1—9 stitches.
Row 42: K1, p2tog, purl to end—8 stitches.
Row 43: Knit to last 3 stitches, k2tog, k1—7 stitches.
Do not bind off. Leave the shoulder stitches on a holder.

SLEEVES (MAKE 2)
Using size 6 (4mm) needles and A, cast on 19 stitches.
Row 1: K1, (p1, k1) to end.
Repeat row 1 twice more.
Row 4: Purl.
Row 5: Knit.
Row 6: Purl.
Repeat rows 5 and 6 6 more times, ending with a wrong-side row.
Bind off.

BLANKET
Front
Using the intarsia method and size 6 (4mm) needles, cast on as follows:
Cast on 9 stitches in B, 9 stitches in A, 9 stitches in C, 9 stitches in D, and 9 stitches in E—45 stitches.
Work the next 72 rows from chart on page 72.
Bind off in seed stitch.

45 stitches

KEY:

☐ Knit on rs, Purl on ws

☒ Purl on rs, Knit on ws

Complex Medium-Sized Bear

KEY:

☒ Knit on rs, Purl on ws using contrasting shade

☐ Knit on rs, Purl on ws

Back

Using size 6 (4mm) needles and A, cast on 45 stitches.

Row 1: K1, (p1, k1) to end.

Repeat row 1 9 more times, ending with a wrong-side row. Working seed stitch border as set by the first 10 rows, continue as follows:

Row 11: Work in seed stitch for 5 stitches, knit to last 5 stitches, work in seed stitch to end.

Row 12: Work in seed stitch for 5 stitches, purl to last 5 stitches, work in seed stitch to end.

Repeat rows 11 and 12 8 more times, ending with a wrong-side row.

Keeping seed stitch border correct as set, work the next 9 rows of the center panel from the chart on page 73, inserting the letters of your choice in one of the contrasting shades.

Next row: Work in seed stitch for 5 stitches, purl to last 5 stitches, work in seed stitch to end.

Next row: Work in seed stitch for 5 stitches, knit to last 5 stitches, work in seed stitch to end.

Next row: Work in seed stitch for 5 stitches, purl to last 5 stitches, work in seed stitch to end.

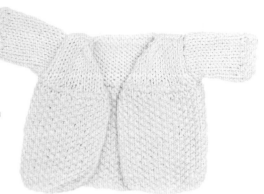

Repeat last 2 rows 7 more times, ending with a wrong-side row.

Next row: K1, (p1, k1) to end.

Repeat last row 9 more times, ending with a wrong-side row.

Bind off in seed stitch.

FINISHING

JACKET

Join both shoulder seams using the three-needle bind-off technique as described on page 26.

Sleeves

Fold sleeve in half lengthwise and mark the center of the bound-off edge with a stitch marker. Line this marker up with the shoulder seam and tack the sleeve in place. Now sew the sleeve to the body. Attach both sleeves in the same way.

Join both side and sleeve seams.

BLANKET

Stitch the front and back pieces together using A.

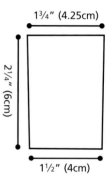

1¾" (4.25cm)

2¼" (6cm)

1½" (4cm)

3¾" (9.5cm)

5" (12.5cm)

5½" (14cm)

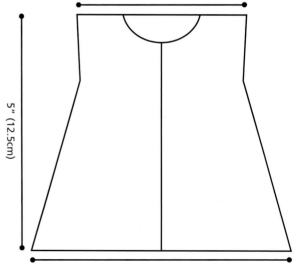

Cowboy Bear

Cowboy Bear is all saddled up and ready for Wild West adventures. With his lasso, cowboy shirt, and chaps, he's certain to become a favorite toy for kids of all ages.

SKILL LEVEL
Intermediate

MATERIALS
For the chaps
- 197 yds (180m) fingering weight yarn
   superfine (A). The bear's outfit on page 76 uses 1 ball Rowan Classic Cashsoft 4ply, 57% extra fine merino, 33% microfiber, 10% cashmere, 1 oz (50g), 215 yds (197m), 441 Walnut

For the neck scarf
- 197 yds (180m) fingering weight yarn
   superfine (B). The bear's outfit on page 76 uses 1 ball Rowan Classic Cashsoft 4ply, 429 Redwood

For the shirt
- 191 yds (175m) fingering weight yarn
   superfine (C). The bear's outfit on page 76 uses 1 ball Rowan 4 ply Soft, 100% Merino wool, 1 oz (50g), 191 yds (175m), 383 Black

For the jeans
- 1 ball Rowan Denim, 100% cotton, 1 oz (50g), 101 yds (93m), 229 Memphis (D)

For the shirt embroidery
- 126 yds (115m) sport weight yarn fine (E). The bear's outfit on page 76 uses small amount Rowan Cotton Glace, 100% cotton, 1 oz (50g), 137 yds (115m), 726 Bleached
- Sizes 3 and 6 (3.25mm and 4mm) needles (or size needed to obtain gauge)
- Tapestry needle
- Approximately 1 yd (almost 1m) length of leather cord
- 5 7mm snaps

GAUGE

JEANS

Before washing:
20 stitches and 28 rows to 4" (10cm) using size 6 (4mm) needles and Denim measured over stockinette stitch.

After washing:
20 stitches and 32 rows to 4" (10cm) using size 6 (4mm) needles and Denim measured over stockinette stitch.

CHAPS/SCARF

28 stitches and 36 rows to 4" (10cm) using size 3 (3.25mm) needles and fingering weight yarn, measured over stockinette stitch.

SHIRT

28 stitches and 36 rows to 4" (10cm) using size 3 (3.25mm) needles and fingering weight yarn, measured over stockinette stitch.

JEANS

Back

Leg (make 2)

Using size 6 (4mm) needles and D, cast on 15 stitches.
Row 1: Knit.
Row 2: Purl.
Repeat rows 1 and 2 until the work measures 6" (15cm) from cast-on edge.
Do not bind off. Leave the stitches on a holder.
Join the 2 legs of the back as follows:
With right sides facing, knit across the 15 stitches of the left leg, then the 15 stitches of the other leg—30 stitches.
Row 1: P14, p2tog, purl to end—29 stitches.
Row 2: K14, p1, k14.
Row 3: P14, k1, p14.
Repeat rows 2 and 3 3 more times, ending with a wrong-side row.
Row 10: K14, p1, k14.
Row 11: Knit.
Row 12: Knit.
Row 13: Purl.
Row 14: Purl.
Bind off.

Front

Leg (make 2)

Using size 6 (4mm) needles and D, cast on 15 stitches.
Row 1: Knit.
Row 2: Purl.
Repeat rows 1 and 2 until the work measures 6" (15cm) from cast-on edge.
Do not bind off. Leave the stitches on a holder.
Join the 2 legs of the front as follows:
With right sides facing, knit across the 15 stitches of the left leg and the 15 stitches of the other leg—30 stitches.
Row 1: P14, p2tog, purl to end—29 stitches.

Row 2: K14, p1, k14.
Row 3: P14, k1, p14.
Row 4: K1, k2togtbl, k11, p1, k11, k2tog, k1—27 stitches.
Row 5: K1, p2tog, p10, k1, p10, p2togtbl, k1—25 stitches.
Row 6: K1, k2togtbl, k9, p1, k9, k2tog, k1—23 stitches.
Row 7: K1, p2tog, p8, k1, p8, p2togtbl, k1—21 stitches.
Row 8: K1, k2togtbl, k7, p1, k7, k2tog, k1—19 stitches.
Row 9: K1, p2tog, p6, k1, p6, p2togtbl, k1—17 stitches.
Row 10: K8, p1, k8.
Do not bind off. Leave the 17 stitches on a holder.

Pocket inserts (make 2)

Using size 6 (4mm) needles and D, cast on 6 stitches.
Row 1: Knit.
Row 2: Purl.
Repeat rows 1 and 2 4 more times, ending with a wrong-side row.
Do not bind off. Leave the stitches on a holder.

Join pocket inserts as follows:
With wrong sides facing, knit across 6 stitches of the right pocket insert, knit across 16 stitches from the front section, and knit across the 6 stitches of the left pocket insert—28 stitches.
Next row: Knit.
Next row: Purl.
Next row: Purl.
Bind off.

Patch pockets (make 2)

Using size 6 (4mm) needles and D, cast on 7 stitches.
Row 1: Purl.

Row 2: K1, p5, k1.
Row 3: Knit.
Row 4: K1, p5, k1.
Repeat rows 3 and 4 3 more times, ending
with a wrong-side row.
Bind off.

CHAPS (MAKE 2)
Using size 3 (3.25mm) needles and A, cast on
27 stitches.
Row 1: K13, sl1, knit to end.
Row 2: K1, purl to last stitch, k1.
Repeat rows 1 and 2 22 more times, ending
with a wrong-side row.
Do not bind off. Leave the stitches on a holder.
Join both chaps as follows:
K13, sl1, k13 across right chap, turn, cast on 7
stitches, turn, k13, sl2, and k13 across left
chap—61 stitches.
Next row: Cast on 7 stitches, purl to end—
68 stitches.
Next row: Cast on 11 stitches, k24, sl1, k33,
sl1, knit to end—79 stitches.
Next row: Purl.
Next row: K35, sl1, k33, sl1, knit to end—
79 stitches.
Next row: Purl.
Bind off.

ANKLE STRAPS (MAKE 2)
Using size 3 (3.25mm) needles and A, work
as follows:
Measure ⅝" (1cm) up the front opening
of the right chap and pick up and knit 4
stitches. Work on these 4 stitches as follows:
Row 1: K1, p2, k1.
Row 2: Knit.
Row 3: K1, p2, k1.
Repeat rows 2 and 3 7 more times, ending
with a wrong-side row.
Bind off.

SHIRT
Back
Using size 3 (3.25mm) needles and C, cast on
29 stitches.
Row 1 (RS): Purl.
Row 2: Knit.
Repeat rows 1 and 2 10 more times, ending
with a wrong-side row.
Row 23: P14, k1, p14.
Row 24: K13, p3, k13.
Row 25: P12, k5, p12.
Row 26: K11, p7, k11.
Row 27: P10, k9, p10.
Row 28: K9, p11, k9.
Row 29: P7, k15, p7.
Row 30: K5, p19, k5.
Row 31: P4, k21, p4.
Row 32: K2, p25, k2.
Row 33: Knit.
Row 34: Purl.
Row 35: Knit.
Row 36: P8, bind off center 13 stitches, p8.
Do not bind off. Leave the 2 sets of shoulder
stitches on a holder.

Right front
Using size 3 (3.25mm) needles and C, cast on
16 stitches.
Row 1: Purl.
Row 2: Knit.
Repeat rows 1 and 2 10 more times, ending
with a wrong-side row.
Row 23: K1, p15.
Row 24: K14, p2.
Row 25: K3, p13.
Row 26: K12, p4.
Row 27: K5, p11.
Row 28: K10, p6.
Row 29: K8, p8.
Row 30: K6, p10.
Row 31: K12, p4.
Row 32: K2, p14.
Row 33: Bind off 6 stitches, knit to end.
Row 34: Purl to last 2 stitches, p2tog.
Row 35: K2tog, knit to end.
Row 36: Purl.
Do not bind off. Leave the shoulder stitches on
a holder.

Left front
Using size 3 (3.25mm) needles and C, cast on
16 stitches.
Row 1: Purl.
Row 2: Knit.
Repeat rows 1 and 2 10 more times, ending
with a wrong-side row.
Row 23: P15, k1.
Row 24: P2, k14.
Row 25: P13, k3.
Row 26: P4, k12.
Row 27: P11, k5.
Row 28: P6, k10.
Row 29: P8, k8.
Row 30: P10, k6.
Row 31: P4, k12.
Row 32: Bind off 6 stitches, p8, k2.

Row 33: Knit to last 2 stitches, k2tog.
Row 34: P2tog, purl to end.
Row 35: Knit.
Row 36: Purl.
Join both shoulder seams using the three-needle bind-off technique (see page 26), then work the collar as follows: Using size 3 (3.25mm) needles and C, and with wrong-side facing, pick up and knit 8 stitches up the left of the neck, 14 stitches across the back, and 8 stitches down the right of the neck—30 stitches.
Row 1: Purl.
Row 2: Knit.
Repeat rows 1 and 2 3 more times, ending with a wrong-side row.
Next row: Purl.
Bind off.

SLEEVES (MAKE 2)
Using size 3 (3.25mm) needles and C, cast on 22 stitches.
Row 1: Purl.
Row 2: Knit.
Repeat rows 1 and 2 12 more times, ending with a wrong-side row.
Bind off.

NECK SCARF
Using size 3 (3.25mm) needles and B, cast on 3 stitches.
Row 1: Purl.
Row 2: K1, m1, k1, m1, k1—5 stitches.
Row 3: Purl.

Row 4: K1, m1, knit to last stitch, m1, k1—7 stitches.
Repeat rows 3 and 4 until there are 17 stitches.
Row 15: K2, (m1, k4 3 times, m1, k3) to end—21 stitches.
Row 16: Purl.
Row 17: Knit.
Row 18: Purl.
Row 19: K3, (m1, k3) to end—27 stitches.
Row 20: Purl.
Row 21: K3, (m1, k3) to end—35 stitches.
Row 22: Cast on 15 stitches, knit to end—50 stitches.
Row 23: Cast on 15 stitches, purl to end—65 stitches.
Bind off.

FINISHING
JEANS
As Rowan Denim shrinks in length when washed for the first time, the front and back sections of the jeans, and enough yarn to sew them up, must be washed following the instructions on the ball band before the jeans are sewn together. If substituting, this may not be the case. Be sure to read your yarn's care instructions.

Join both front and back sections of the jeans as follows: Sew the outer side seams. Start at the top (bind-off edge) and work down to the bottom (cast-on edge). Now, join the inner leg seams. Starting at the cast-on edge of the right leg, work up to the top, and then work down the corresponding seam of the left leg.

Whip stitch the pocket inserts into place on the inside of the jeans. Stitch the patch pockets to the outside of the back of the jeans at the top of each leg. Around the waistband, sew vertical straight stitches to form belt loops. Cut a length of yarn and thread this around the waistband, under the belt loops. This length of yarn can be pulled to fit the waist of the bear snugly.

SHIRT
Sleeves: Fold sleeve in half lengthwise and mark the center of the bound-off edge with a stitch marker. Line this marker up with the shoulder seam and tack the sleeve in place. Now sew the sleeve to the body. Attach both sleeves in the same way. Join both side and sleeve seams.

Sew snaps to the front opening, positioning one just below the neck, one just above the cast-on edge, and the other in between.

CHAPS
Sew one half of a snap to the wrong side of each ankle strap at the bound-off edge. Using the photograph as a guide, stretch the strap around the leg and mark a suitable position for the corresponding half of the snap. Sew in place.

The right-hand side of the waistband is slightly longer than the left (where you cast on 11 stitches) and it's on this end that you are going to sew the final snap—sew one half of the snap to the wrong side of this longer band and sew the corresponding half of the snap to the right side of the waistband so that the chaps fit snugly around the bear's waist, over the jeans.

Embroidery: The shirt has stockinette stitch detailing across the shoulders (front and back) which is in contrast to the reverse stockinette stitch of the main shirt. To highlight this further, use E and a large tapestry needle to create a running stitch which forms a border around this detailing. In the same way, embroider a breast pocket on both the right and left fronts.

LASSO
The leather cord is to be used as Cowboy Bear's lasso. This can be worn as shown or coiled around and worn over his arm or shoulder.

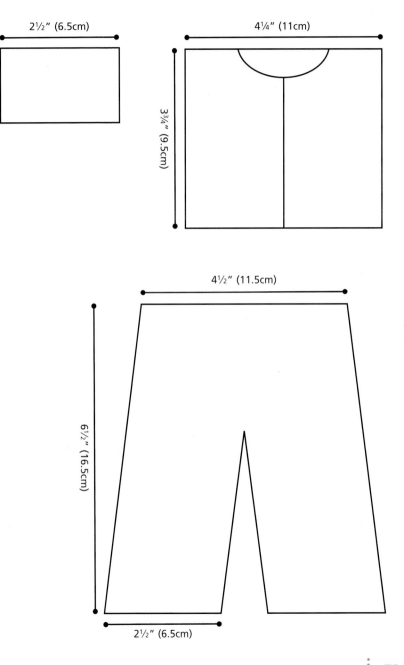

Complex Large Bear

With its two-tone coloring and jointed arms and legs, you can't help falling in love with this large teddy. This pattern is ideal for more advanced knitters and creates a truly adorable bear.

FINISHED SIZE
Height: 13¾" (35cm)
Diameter (around body): 11⅞" (30cm)

MATERIALS
Option A (Beige contrast)
- 191 yds (175m) DK weight yarn **(3)** light used double throughout (A). The bear on page 87 uses 2 balls Rowan Felted Tweed, 50% Merino wool, 25% alpaca, 25% viscose/rayon, 1 oz (50g), 191 yds (175m), 157 Camel
- 142 yds (130m) DK weight yarn **(3)** light (B). The bear on page 87 uses 1 ball Rowan Cashsoft DK, 57% extra fine merino, 33% microfiber, 10% cashmere, 1 oz (50g), 142 yds (130m), 507 Savannah

Option B (Cream contrast)
- 191 yds (175m) DK weight yarn **(3)** light used double throughout (A). The bear on page 82 uses 2 balls Rowan Felted Tweed, 50% Merino wool, 25% alpaca, 25% viscose/rayon, 1 oz (50g), 191 yds (175m), 156 Wheat
- 142 yds (130m) DK weight yarn **(3)** light (B). The bear on page 82 uses 1 ball Rowan Cashsoft DK, 57% extra fine merino, 33% microfiber, 10% cashmere, 1 oz (50g), 142 yds (130m), 500 Cream
- Sizes 6 and 7 (4mm and 4.5mm) needles (or size needed to obtain gauge)
- 175 yds (160m) sport weight yarn **(2)** fine for facial features. The bear on page 82 uses small amount Rowan Calmer, 75% cotton, 25% acrylic, 1 oz (50g), 175 yds (160m), 481 Coffee Bean

- 4 white plastic ⅝" (16mm) teddy bear joints
- 3 oz (85g) toy stuffing

GAUGE
20 stitches and 30 rows to 4" (10cm) using size 6 (4mm) needles and DK weight yarn (used double) measured over stockinette stitch.

BODY
Sides (make 2)
Using size 7 (4.5mm) needles and A (used double), cast on 9 stitches. Work as for knitting the body until * on page 62.
Repeat rows 18 and 19 10 more times ending with a right-side row.
Row 42: Knit.
Row 43: P9, p2tog, p1, p2togtbl, purl to end —21 stitches.
Row 44: Knit.
Row 45: P8, p2tog, p1, p2togtbl, purl to end—19 stitches.
Row 46: K7, k2togtbl, k1, k2tog, knit to end—17 stitches.
Row 47: P6, p2tog, p1, p2togtbl, purl to end—15 stitches.
Row 48: K5, k2togtbl, k1, k2tog, knit to end—13 stitches.
Row 49: P4, p2tog, p1, p2togtbl, purl to end—11 stitches.
Row 50: K3, k2togtbl, k1, k2tog, knit to end—9 stitches.
Row 51: (P2tog) 4 times, k1—5 stitches.
Do not bind off. Thread yarn through the remaining stitches, pull together, and secure.

HEAD
Left side
Using size 6 (4mm) needles and A (used double), cast on 13 stitches. Work as for knitting the left side of the head on page 62.

Right side
Using size 6 (4mm) needles and A (used double), cast on 13 stitches. Work as for knitting the right side of the head on page 63.

Head gusset
Using size 6 (4mm) needles and A (used double), cast on 4 stitches. Work as for knitting the head gusset on page 63.

LEGS (MAKE 2)
Using size 6 (4mm) needles and A (used double), cast on 17 stitches. Work as for knitting the legs on page 63.

FEET PADS (MAKE 2)
Using size 6 (4mm) needles B, cast on 3 stitches. Work as for knitting the feet pads on page 64.

ARMS
Inner arms (make 2)
Using size 6 (4mm) needles and B, cast on 3 stitches. Work as for knitting the inner arms on page 64. **Remember to use yarn A doubled when changing yarns.**

Outer arms (make 2)
Using size 6 (4mm) needles and A (used double), cast on 3 stitches. Work as for knitting the outer arms on page 64.

Ears (make 2)

Using size 6 (4mm) needles and B, cast on 7 stitches.

Row 1: Knit.

Row 2: K1, p5, k1.

Repeat rows 1 and 2 once more.

Row 5: K2tog, knit to last 2 stitches, k2tog—5 stitches.

Bind off and, **at the same time**, k2tog at each end of the bound-off row. Leave a long enough tail to shape ear and attach it to the head.

FINISHING

HEAD

Work as for finishing the head on page 64.

FACIAL FEATURES

Using the brown yarn (Rowan Calmer shade 481), sew the bear's facial features as follows:

Eyes

Work as for finishing the eyes on page 64.

Nose and mouth

Work as for finishing the nose and mouth on page 65.

BODY

Sew the 2 pieces together as follows (the seams are at the center front and center back of the body): Starting at the cast-on edge, sew the first seam all the way to the top of the body. Sew the other seam in the same way but stop approximately ⅔ of the way up. Join the cast-on edges of the 2 pieces. Using the opening that you have left, insert the shank half of the joints for the legs and arms. Use the shaping on the body as a guide–for the legs, position the joints approximately ⅜" (1cm) up from the start of the side shaping, and for the

arms, position the joints at the beginning of shoulder shaping. Then stuff the body until it is firm and roughly 7¾" (20cm) in diameter (using the photograph as a guide to help you to achieve a good shape). Sew up the remaining ⅓ of the second seam. Fasten securely.

You may want to put some of the stuffing in before you position your joints so that you can see the shape better—do whatever works best for your bear.

ARMS

Each arm has an outer section and inner section. The inner section has a paw pad in the contrasting yarn. Join the inner section to the outer section starting at the top of the arm, working down one side and then up the other, stopping approximately ⅔ of the way up. Position the arm so that the top of the inner section meets the shank of the shoulder joint (level with the shoulder). When you are happy with the positioning, push the shank through the knitted fabric and secure inside the arm with the washer half of the joint. Then, using the opening you have left, stuff the arm until it is firm, then sew up the remaining ⅓ of the seam. Fasten securely.

LEGS

Each leg has been knitted in 1 piece, and will have a foot pad attached at the sole. Fold the leg in half lengthwise and sew the 2 cast-on edges together ⅔ of the way so that you leave an opening, forming a seam that runs down the back of the leg. When folding the length in half, you will have folded the cast-on edge in half too—join these 2 edges together, creating

a seam that runs across the top of the leg from front to back. Position the leg so that the top of the inside leg meets up with the shank of the leg joint. When you are happy with the positioning, push the shank through the knitted fabric and secure inside the leg with the washer half of the joint. Now firmly stuff the leg and sew up the opening, then attach the foot pad by sewing around the edges of the pad, joining it to the bound-off edge of the leg.

Ears

Work as for finishing the ears on page 65.

ASSEMBLING YOUR BEAR

Your bear's arms and legs have been attached with joints, and so all that remains is to attach the head. Sew the head securely to the top center of the body.

First Birthday Bear

Celebrate an important milestone with First Birthday Bear. Dressed in pink for a girl or blue for a boy, and complete with a little birthday cupcake, this bear is sure to bring a touch of magic to your little one's special day.

SKILL LEVEL
Intermediate

MATERIALS
For the sweater
Boy's version
- 186 yds (170m) worsted weight yarn **(4)** medium (A). The bear's outfit opposite uses 2 balls Rowan Handknit Cotton, 100% cotton, 1 oz (50g), 93 yds (85m), 327 Aqua

Girl's version
- 186 yds (170m) worsted weight yarn **(4)** medium (B). The bear's outfit opposite uses 2 balls Rowan Handknit Cotton, 332 Rose

For the hat trim
- 186 yds (170m) worsted weight yarn **(4)** medium (C). The bear's outfit opposite uses 1 ball Rowan Handknit Cotton, 263 Bleached
- 40" (approximately 1m) silver curling ribbon
- 16" (40.5cm) white elastic

Boy and Girl
- Sizes 2, 3, 5, and 6 (2.75mm, 3.25mm, 3.75mm, and 4mm) needles (or size needed to obtain gauge)
- Tapestry needle
- Sewing thread

For the cupcake
- 126 yds (115m) sport weight yarn **(2)** fine (D). The cake on page 85 uses 1 ball Rowan Cotton Glace, 100% cotton, 1 oz (50g), 137 yds (115m), 725 Ecru
- 123 yds (113m) DK weight yarn **(3)** light (E). The cake on page 85 uses 1 ball Rowan Wool Cotton, 50% wool, 50% cotton, 1 oz (50g), 123 yds (113m), 929 Dream

- Small amount of worsted weight yarn **(4)** medium (F). The cupcakes on page 85 use small amounts of Rowan Handknit Cotton, 327 Aqua and 310 Shell, for icing
- Small amount of sport weight yarn **(2)** fine. The cupcake on page 85 use small amounts Rowan Cotton Glace shades 726 Bleached (G) and 833 Ochre (H), for candle
- Approximately 23 3mm white beads, such as Rowan 01016 for cupcake with beads
- Size 3 (3.25mm) double-pointed needles (or size needed to obtain gauge)
- Small amount of toy stuffing
- Tapestry needle

GAUGE
20 stitches and 28 rows to 4" (10cm) using size 6 (4mm) needles and worsted weight yarn, measured over stockinette stitch.

SWEATER
Back
Using size 3 (3.25mm) needles and A for boy's version or B for girl's version, cast on 33 stitches.
Row 1: K1, (p1, k1) to end.
Repeat row 1 3 more times, ending with a wrong-side row.
Change to size 6 (4mm) needles
Row 5: Knit.
Row 6: Purl.
Repeat rows 5 and 6 14 more times, ending with a wrong-side row.
Next row: K6, bind off center 21 stitches, k6.
Do not bind off. Leave both sets of shoulder stitches on holders.

Front
Using size 3 (3.25mm) needles and A for boy's version or B for girl's version, cast on 33 stitches.
Row 1: K1, (p1, k1) to end.
Repeat row 1 3 more times, ending with a wrong-side row.
Change to size 6 (4mm) needles
Row 5: Knit.
Row 6: Purl.
Repeat rows rows 5 and 6 10 more times, ending with a wrong-side row.
Row 27: K12, turn and work on these 12 stitches only as follows:
Row 28: Purl.
Row 29: Knit to last 3 stitches, k2tog, k1—11 stitches.
Row 30: P1, p2tog, purl to end—10 stitches.
Repeat rows 29 and 30 until 6 stitches remain.
Row 35: Knit.
Row 36: Purl.
Do not bind off. Leave the shoulder stitches on a holder.
With right side facing, rejoin yarn to remaining stitches and work as follows:
Next row: Bind off center 9 stitches, knit to end.
Row 28: Purl.
Row 29: K1, k2togtbl, knit to end—11 stitches.
Row 30: Purl to last 3 stitches, p2togtbl, p1—10 stitches.
Repeat rows 29 and 30 until 6 stitches remain.
Row 35: Knit.
Row 36: Purl.
Do not bind off. Leave the shoulder stitches on a holder.

NECKBAND

Join the right shoulder using the three-needle bind-off technique as described on page 26. With right side facing, using size 6 (4mm) needles and A for boy's version or B for girl's version, pick up and knit 10 stitches down the left front of the neck, 9 stitches across the center front, 10 stitches up the right front of the neck, and 22 stitches across the back—51 stitches.

Row 1: K1, (p1, k1) to end.
Repeat row 1 once more.
Bind off in seed stitch.

Sleeves (make 2)

Using size 3 (3.25mm) needles and A for boy's version or B for girl's version, cast on 25 stitches.

Row 1: K1, (p1, k1) to end
Repeat row 1 3 more times, ending with a wrong-side row.

Change to size 6 (4mm) needles.
Row 5: Knit.
Row 6: Purl.
Repeat rows 5 and 6 3 more times, ending with a wrong-side row.
Bind off.

PARTY HAT

Using size 3 (3.25mm) needles and C, cast on 29 stitches.

Row 1: Knit.
Row 2: Knit.
Change to size 6 (4mm) needles and A for boy's version or B for girl's version.
Row 3: Knit.
Row 4: Purl.
Row 5: Knit.
Row 6: Purl.
Row 7: K2tog, knit to last 2 stitches, k2tog—27 stitches.
Row 8: Purl.

Repeat rows 7 and 8 until 19 stitches remain, ending with a wrong-side row.
Next row: K2tog, knit to last 2 stitches, k2tog.
Next row: P2tog, purl to last 2 stitches, p2tog.
Repeat last 2 rows until 3 stitches remain.
Next row: K3tog.
Fasten off.

CUPCAKE

Cupcake holder—side

Using size 6 (4mm) needles and D, cast on 42 stitches.
Row 1: K2, (p1, k1) to last 2 stitches, p2.
Repeat row 1 once more.
Change to size 3 (3.25mm) needles.
Repeat row 1 6 more times, ending with a wrong-side row.
Change to size 2 (2.75mm) needles.
Repeat row 1 until work measures 2" (5cm) from cast-on edge, ending with a wrong-side row.
Bind off.

Cupcake holder—base

Using size 2 (2.75mm) needles and D, cast on 5 stitches.
Row 1: Purl.
Row 2: K1, m1, k3, m1, k1—7 stitches.
Row 3: Purl.
Row 4: K1, m1, k5, m1, k1—9 stitches.
Row 5: Purl.
Row 6: K1, m1, k7, m1, k1—11 stitches.
Row 7: Purl.
Row 8: Knit.
Row 9: Purl.
Row 10: K2togtbl, k7, k2togtbl—9 stitches.
Row 11: Purl.
Row 12: K2togtbl, k5, k2togtbl—7 stitches.
Row 13: Purl.
Row 14: K2togtbl, k3, k2togtbl—5 stitches.
Row 15: Purl.
Bind off.

Cupcake

Using size 5 (3.75mm) needles and E, cast on 10 stitches.

Row 1: Purl.
Row 2: K2, m1, k1, m1, k1, m1, k2, m1, k1, m1, k1, m1, k2—16 stitches.
Row 3: Purl.
Row 4: Knit.
Row 5: Purl.
Row 6: K1, (m1, k2) to last stitch, m1, k1—24 stitches.
Row 7: Purl.
Row 8: Knit.
Repeat rows 7 and 8 4 more times, and then row 7 once more.
Row 18: K2tog, (k1, k2tog) to last 2 stitches, k2—17 stitches.
Row 19: Purl.
Row 20: Knit.
Row 21: Purl.
Row 22: K2tog, k2, (k2tog) to last stitch, k1—10 stitches.
Row 23: Purl.
Bind off.

Icing

Using size 2 (2.75mm) needles and F (in the shade of your choice, cast on 5 stitches.

Row 1: K1, p3, k1.
Row 2: K1, m1, k3, m1, k1—7 stitches.
Row 3: K1, p5, k1.
Row 4: K1, m1, k5, m1, k1—9 stitches.
Row 5: K1, p7, k1.
Row 6: K1, m1, k7, m1, k1—11 stitches.
Row 7: K1, p9, k1.
Row 8: Knit.
Row 9: K1, p9, k1.
Row 10: K2togtbl, k7, k2togtbl—9 stitches.
Row 11: K1, p7, k1.
Row 12: K2togtbl, k5, k2togtbl—7 stitches.
Row 13: K1, p5, k1.
Row 14: K2togtbl, k3, k2togtbl—5 stitches.

Row 15: K1, p3, k1.
Bind off.

Candle

Using the technique described below, make the candle out of an I-cord as follows:
Using size 3 (3.25mm) double-pointed needles and G, cast on 3 stitches
Row 1: Knit.
Repeat row 1 until cord is 1⅝" (4cm).
Break off yarn, thread through remaining stitches and pull together.

Technique for making I-cord: Once you have cast on your stitches, knit one row. You would now usually turn your needles but to make the cord, do not turn. Instead, slide the stitches to the other end of the double-pointed needle, ready to be knitted again. The yarn will now be at the left edge of the knitting and so, to knit, you must pull it tightly across the back of your work and then knit one row. You continue in this way, never turning and always sliding the work to the other end of the double-pointed needle, and the right side of the work will always be facing you.

Flame

Using size 3 (3.25mm) needles and H, cast on 3 stitches.

Row 1: K1, p1, k1.
Row 2: K1, m1, k1, m1, k1—5 stitches.
Row 3: K1, p3, k1.
Row 4: K1, sl2, k1, p2sso, k1—3 stitches.
Row 5: Sl2, k1, p2sso—1 stitch.
Fasten off, leaving a long tail.

FINISHING

SWEATER

Join the left shoulder seam using the three-needle bind-off technique as described on page 26.

Sleeves

Fold sleeve in half lengthwise and mark the center of the bound-off edge with a stitch marker. Line this marker up with the shoulder seam and tack the sleeve in place. Now sew the sleeve to the body. Attach both sleeves in the same way.
Join both side and sleeve seams.

PARTY HAT

Sew the side seams together by starting at the cast-on edge and working up to the point of the hat, creating a seam at the back.

Using the photograph as a guide, embroider a number 1 using duplicate stitch on the center front of the hat. Attach 2 10" (25cm) lengths of curling ribbon to the point of the hat.

Sew each end of an 8" (20.5cm) length of white elastic to each side of the hat, inside the cast-on edge.

CUPCAKE

Sew together the 2 side seams of the cupcake holder. Join the sides of the holder to the base by stitching the edge of the base to the bound-off edge of the sides. Fill the holder with stuffing and then insert the cupcake onto the top of this so that the edges of the cake sit just inside the top of the case. You may want to put a bit more stuffing in or take a bit out, depending on the shape. When you are happy with the shape of the cupcake, whip stitch the edges of the cupcake inside the rim of the holder. Stitch the icing to the top of the cupcake.

Cupcake with candle

Thread the long tail that was left after fastening off the flame onto a tapestry needle. Stitch the flame to the top of the candle and then thread the yarn down through the center of the knitted I-cord and out through the bottom. Stitch the base of the candle to the top of the cake.

Cupcake with pearls

Using a fine sewing needle and thread, stitch the beads in a random fashion to the top of the icing.

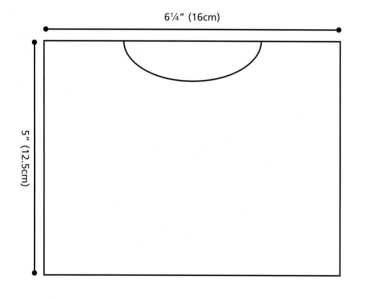

6¼" (16cm)

5" (12.5cm)

2½" (6.5cm)

1¾" (4.25cm)

SKILL LEVEL
Simple

MATERIALS
For the bikini
- 123 yds (113m) DK weight yarn **3** light. The bear's outfit on this page uses 1 ball Rowan Wool Cotton, 50% wool, 50% cotton, 1 oz (50g), 123 yds (113m), 943 Flower
- Size 6 (4mm) needles (or size needed to obtain gauge)
- 6 8mm pink beads
- 1 7mm snap
- Tapestry needle

GAUGE
22 stitches and 30 rows to 4" (10cm) using size 6 (4mm) needles and DK weight yarn, measured over stockinette stitch.

BIKINI TOP (MAKE 2)
Using size 6 (4mm) needles, cast on 15 stitches.
Row 1: Purl.
Repeat row 1 once more.
Row 3: K2, yo, k2tog, (k1, yo, k2tog) to last 2 stitches, k2.
Row 4: Knit.
Row 5: Knit.
Row 6: K1, purl to last stitch, k1.
Row 7: K1, k2togtbl, knit to last 3 stitches, k2tog, k1—13 stitches.
Repeat rows 6 and 7 until 5 stitches remain.
Next row: K1, p3, k1.
Next row: K1, sl2, k1, p2sso, k1—3 stitches.
Next row: K1, p1, k1.

Swimmer Bear

In her adorable little bikini, Swimmer Bear is all ready to soak up the sun on vacation.

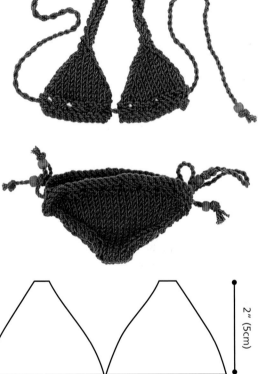

Next row: Knit.
Repeat last 2 rows until work measures 5⅛" (13cm) from cast-on edge.
Bind off.

BIKINI BOTTOMS (MAKE 2)
Using size 6 (4mm) needles, cast on 27 stitches.
Row 1: Purl.
Row 2: Purl.
Row 3: K2, yo, k2tog, (k1, yo, k2tog) to last 2 stitches, k2.
Row 4: Knit.
Row 5: Knit.
Row 6: K1, purl to last stitch, k1.
Row 7: K1, k2togtbl, knit to last 3 stitches, k2tog, k1—25 stitches.
Repeat rows 6 and 7 until 19 stitches remain.
Next row: K1, p2tog, purl to last 3 stitches, k2tog, k1—17 stitches.
Next row: K1, k2togtbl, knit to last 3 stitches, k2tog, k1—15 stitches.
Repeat last 2 rows until 7 stitches remain.
Next row: K1, purl to last stitch, k1.
Next row: Knit.
Next row: K1, purl to last stitch, k1.
Do not bind off. Leave the stitches on a holder.

FINISHING
BIKINI TOP
Sew one half of the snap to the wrong side of the bound-off end of the left strap, and the other half of the snap to the right side of the bound-off end of the right strap.

BIKINI BOTTOMS
Join the 2 halves of the bikini bottoms using the three-needle bind-off technique as described on page 26.
Make twisted cords as follows:

Medium length (make 2)
Cut 2 strands of yarn approximately 50" (125cm) in length. Take the strands of yarn and secure at each end with knots. Ask someone to help you and give them one end of the yarn while you hold the other. With the yarn outstretched, twist each end in opposite directions until it shows signs of twisting back on itself. Bring the 2 ends of the cord together and hold tightly, allowing the 2 halves to twist together. Smooth out any bumps by running your fingers up and down the cord. You will now have a twisted cord measuring approximately 20" (50cm).

Longer length (make 1)
Work as for the medium length cord but start with strands measuring approximately 70" (175cm). You will end with a cord that is approximately 27½" (70cm).

Thread a bead onto each end of the 3 cords and secure with a knot.

Thread the longer cord through the eyelets of each section of the bikini top and tie at the back.

Thread one of the medium lengths of cord through the eyelets of one of the sections of the bikini bottoms, then the other cord through the other section. Cords will tie at the sides.

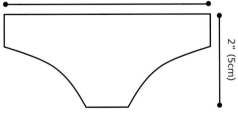

2" (5cm)

5½" (13.5cm)

4½" (11.5cm)

2" (5cm)

Golfer Bear

Perfect for sports fans, Golfer Bear is all dressed and ready to tee off. His smart Fair Isle sweater will be the envy of everyone on the green!

SKILL LEVEL
Advanced

MATERIALS
For the tank top
- 120 yds (110m) fingering weight yarn **(1)** superfine (A). The bear's outfit opposite uses 1 ball Rowan Scottish Tweed 4ply, 100% wool, 1 oz (50g), 120 yds (110m), 025 Oatmeal
- 191 yds (175m) fingering weight yarn **(1)** superfine (B). The bear's outfit opposite uses 1 ball Rowan 4 ply Soft, 100% Merino wool, 1 oz (50g), 191 yds (175m), 372 Sooty
- 120 yds (110m) fingering weight yarn **(1)** superfine (C). The bear's outfit opposite uses 1 ball Rowan Scottish Tweed 4ply, 015 Apple

For the tank top and visor
- 120 yds (110m) fingering weight yarn **(1)** superfine (D). The bear's outfit opposite uses 1 ball Rowan Scottish Tweed 4ply, 017 Lobster
- 197 yds (180m) fingering weight yarn **(1)** superfine (E). The bear's outfit opposite uses 1 ball Rowan Classic Cashsoft 4ply, 57% extra fine merino, 33% microfiber, 10% cashmere, 1 oz (50g), 215 yds (197m), 433 Cream

For the pants
- 123 yds (113m) fingering weight yarn **(1)** superfine (F). The bear's outfit opposite uses 1 ball Rowan Wool Cotton, 50% wool, 50% cotton, 1¾ oz (50g), 123 yds (113m), 963 Smalt

- Sizes 3 and 6 (3.25mm and 4mm) needles (or size needed to obtain gauge)
- 1 7mm snap
- Tapestry needle

GAUGE
PANTS
22 stitches and 30 rows to 4" (10cm) using size 6 (4mm) needles and fingering weight yarn, measured over stockinette stitch.

TANK TOP
28 stitches and 36 rows to 4" (10cm) using size 3 (3.25mm) needles and fingering weight yarn, measured over stockinette stitch.

PANTS
Front
Leg (make 2)
Using size 3 (3.25mm) needles and F, cast on 17 stitches.
Row 1: K1, (p1, k1) to end.
Row 2: P1, (k1, p1) to end.
Repeat rows 1 and 2 once more.
Change to size 6 (4mm) needles.
Row 5: K1, m1, (k5, m1) 3 times, k1—21 stitches.
Row 6: Purl.
Row 7: Knit.
Row 8: Purl.
Repeat rows 7 and 8 8 more times.
Do not bind off. Leave the stitches on a holder.
Join the 2 legs of the front section as follows:

With right sides facing and using size 3 (3.25mm) needles, knit across 20 stitches of the left leg, knit the last stitch of the left leg together with the first stitch of the right leg, knit to end—41 stitches.
Row 1: Purl.
Row 2: K5, k2tog, (k3, k2tog) to last 4 stitches, k4—34 stitches.
Row 3: Purl.
Row 4: Knit.
Row 5: Purl.
Repeat rows 4 and 5 7 more times, ending with right-side row.
Next row: (K1, p1) to end.
Repeat last row 3 more times, ending with a wrong-side row.
Bind off in rib pattern.

Back
Work as for the Front.

TANK TOP
Front
Using size 3 (3.25mm) needles and E, cast on 48 stitches.

Row 1: (K1, p1) to end.

Repeat row 1 3 more times, ending with a wrong-side row.

Starting with a right-side row, work the next 28 rows from the chart on page 90.

Next, working in A only, continue as follows:

Next row: Bind off 6 stitches, k18, turn and work on these 18 stitches only as follows:

Next row: Bind off 1 stitch, purl to end—17 stitches.

Next row: Knit to last 3 stitches, k2tog, k1—16 stitches.

Next row: K1, p2tog, purl to end—15 stitches.

Repeat last 2 rows until 7 stitches remain.

Bind off.

Rejoin yarn to remaining stitches and work as follows:

Next row: Bind off 1 stitch, knit to end.

Next row: Bind off 6 stitches, purl to last 3 stitches, p2togtbl, k1end—17 stitches.

Next row: K1, k2togtbl, knit to end—16 stitches.

Next row: Purl to last 3 stitchess, p2togtbl, k1—15 stitches.

Repeat last 2 rows until 7 stitches remain.

Do not bind off. Leave these shoulder stitches on a holder.

Back
Using size 3 (3.25mm) needles and E, cast on 48 stitches.

Row 1: (K1, p1) to end.

Repeat row 1 3 more times, ending with a wrong-side row.

Change to yarn A.

Row 5: Knit.

Row 6: Purl.

Repeat rows 5 and 6 13 more times, ending with a wrong-side row.

Row 33: Bind off 6 stitches, knit to end—42 stitches.

Row 34: Bind off 6 stitches, purl to end—36 stitches.

Row 35: Knit.

Row 36: Purl.

Repeat rows 35 and 36 4 more times, ending with a wrong-side row.

Row 41: K7, bind off center 22 stitches, k7.

Slip the first set of 7 stitches (right shoulder) onto a holder and work on the second set of 7 stitches (left shoulder) as follows:

Next row: Purl.

Next row: Knit.

Repeat the last 2 rows once more, ending with a wrong-side row.

Bind off.

NECKBAND
Join the right shoulder using the three-needle bind-off technique as described on page 26. With right sides facing, using size 3 (3.25mm) needles and E, pick up and knit 12 stitches down the left front of the neck, 12 stitches up the right front of the neck, and 24 stitches across the back—48 stitches.

Row 1: (K1, p1) to end.

Bind off loosely in rib pattern.

VISOR
Peak
Using size 6 (4mm) needles and D (with the yarn doubled), cast on 7 stitches.

Row 1: Purl.

Row 2: K1, (m1, k1) to end—13 stitches.

Row 3: Purl.

Row 4: K1, (m1, k1) to end—25 stitches.

Row 5: Purl.

Row 6: Knit.

Row 7: Purl.

Row 8: K5, (m1, k5) to end—29 stitches.

Row 9: Purl.

Row 10: Knit.

Row 11: Purl.

Bind off.

Headband
Using size 6 (4mm) needles and E (with the yarn doubled), pick up and knit 9 stitches along the right edge of the peak, 4 stitches along the center (the curve), and 9 stitches along the left edge of the peak—22 stitches.

Work as follows:

Next row: Cast on 18 stitches, purl to end.

Next row: Cast on 18 stitches, k40, wrap next

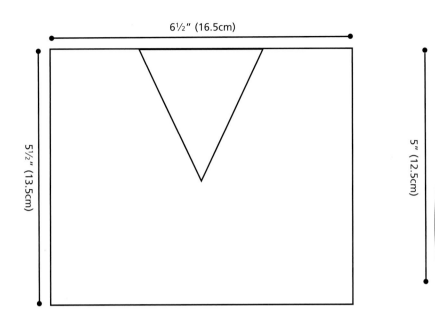

stitch and turn.
Next row: P22, wrap next stitch and turn.
Next row: Knit to end.
Bind off.

FINISHING
PANTS
Join both the front and back sections of the
pants as follows: Sew the outer side seams.
Start at the top (bound-off edge) and work
down to the bottom (cast-on edge). Now join
the inner leg seams. Starting at the cast-on
edge of the right leg, work up to the top, and
then work down the corresponding seam of
the left leg.

TANK TOP
The left shoulder has been left open to make it
easier to pull off and on over the bear's head.
Sew one half of the snap to the right side of
the back shoulder, and the other half to the
wrong side of the front shoulder and fasten.
Armhole edgings: Using size 3 (3.25mm)
needles and E, pick up and knit 34 stitches
around armhole edge. Bind off loosely.
Note: Take extra care when picking up the left
armhole band as the shoulder is only joined by
the snap—make sure the front shoulder is
overlapping the back as you pick up.

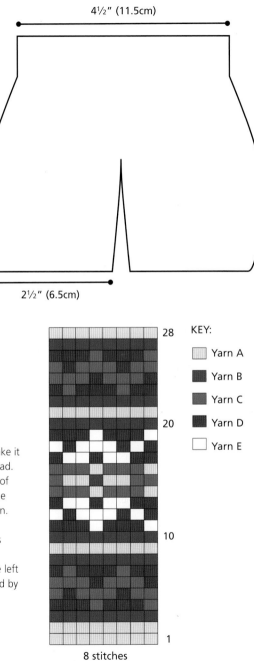

KEY:

☐ Yarn A
■ Yarn B
■ Yarn C
■ Yarn D
☐ Yarn E

8 stitches

YARN AND GAUGE

QUANTITIES OF YARN AND DYE LOTS

At the beginning of each project the quantities of yarn are given. If different yarns are used, these quantities may alter. This is because the length of a ball of yarn depends on its weight and fiber content. If you are substituting yarns, you must check for the following things:

Check the gauge of your preferred yarn against the gauge of the pattern (the gauge of the yarn can be found on the ball band and the gauge of the pattern can be found at the beginning of the instructions). These must be the same if the substitution is to be successful.

Check the length of a ball of your preferred yarn against the length of a ball of the recommended yarn. The reason for this is that the weight of a ball of yarn varies between types. Therefore, you cannot rely on the weight to give you the correct amount of yarn—you must compare length.

If more than one ball of a particular color is needed (for the basic bears, for example), ensure that you buy them from the same dye lot. The color of a specific shade of yarn can vary between dye lots and the change will show in the finished project.

GAUGE

Gauge can differ quite dramatically between knitters. This is because of the way that the needles and yarn are held. If your gauge does not match that stated in the pattern, you should change your needle size following this simple rule:

If your knitting is too loose (fewer stitches and rows than the gauge stated), you must use a smaller needle to make your knitting tighter. If your knitting is too tight (more stitches and rows than the gauge stated), you must use a bigger needle to make your knitting looser. It is important that your gauge is correct to ensure that the outfits fit your bear.

ABBREVIATIONS

PB Place Bead: bring the yarn forward, slip bead to front of work, slip 1 st purlwise, take yarn to back of work. Bead will now be sitting in front of the slipped stitch.

P2B Place two beads: bring the yarn forward, slip two beads to front of work, slip 1 st purlwise, take yarn to back of work. Beads will now be sitting in front of the slipped stitch.

PS Place Sequin: bring the yarn forward, slip sequin to front of work, slip 1 st purlwise, take yarn to back of work. Sequin will now be sitting in front of the slipped stitch.

ML Place sequin on a loop: knit into the next stitch and, before slipping the stitch off the left needle, slide a sequin up to the needle and bring the yarn to the front of the work between the needle points. Wrap the yarn around your left thumb and take it back between the needle points. Now, knit into the stitch again and then slip the stitch off the needle. You will now have two stitches on the right-hand needle. Bind one off by lifting one stitch over the other.

C6B Cable six back: Slip the next 3sts onto cable needle and hold at back of work, k3 from left needle and then knit the 3sts from the cable needle

wrap st Wrap stitch: Slip the next stitch from the left to the right needle, bring the yarn forward between the needle points, slip the slipped stitch back onto the left needle and take the yarn to the back again.

k	knit
p	purl
rs	right side
ws	wrong side
k2tog	knit two stitches together
p2tog	purl two stitches together
k3tog	knit three stitches together
p3tog	purl three stitches together
k2togtbl	knit two stitches together through back of loop
p2togtbl	purl two stitches together through back of loop
m1	make one stitch
yo	yarn over
ybk	yarn back
yfwd	yarn forward
sl1	slip one stitch
sl2	slip two stitches
p2sso	pass two slipped stitches over

Intarsia Intarsia knitting produces a single thickness fabric that uses different balls of yarn for different areas of color. There should be very little, if any, carrying across of yarns at the back of the work.

There are several ways to keep the separate colors of yarn organized when working in intarsia. My preferred method is to use yarn bobbins. Small amounts of yarn can be wound onto bobbins, which should then be kept close to the back of the work while knitting, and only unwound when more yarn is needed.

RESOURCES

Rowan yarns are widely distributed. To find a store near you, contact Westminster Fibers, Inc. (see below) or visit the Rowan website at www.knitrowan.com.

Westminster Fibers, Inc.
165 Ledge Street
Nashua, NH 03080
www.westminsterfibers.com
(603) 886-5041/5043

Fingering or Sock Yarn
Naturespun Wool or Cotton Fine by Brown Sheep
Brown Sheep Yarn Company
100662 Country Road 16
Mitchell, NE 69357
www.brownsheep.com
(800) 826-9136

Baby Ull by Dale of Norway
Dale of Norway Inc.
4750 Shelburne Road, Suite 20
Shelburne, VT 05482
www.dale.no
(802) 383-0132

DK or Light Worsted Weight Yarns
Babysoft by Lion Brand
Lion Brand Yarn Co.
135 Kero Road
Carlstadt, NJ 07072
www.lionbrand.com
(800) 795-5466

Plymouth Encore DK
Plymouth Yarn Company
500 Lafayette Street
Bristol, PA 19007
www.plymouthyarn.com
(215) 788-0459

Provence by Classic Elite
Classic Elite Yarns
300 Jackson Street
Lowell, MA 01852
(978) 453-2837
www.classiceliteyarns.com

Teddy Bear Joints
CR's Crafts
www.crscraft.com
(641) 567-2878

Sassy Bears and Fabrics
www.sassybearsandfabrics.com

Stockade Wood and Craft Supply
www.stockade.ca
(800) 463-0920

Sunshine Discount Crafts
www.sunshinecrafts.com
(800) 729-2878

yarn standards

The Yarn Council of America have a system of categorizing yarns that you may find useful. It provides a guide only and you should always use the gauge and needle size given in a pattern you are following.

yarn weight symbol	yarn category names	recommended US (metric) needle size	gauge range in stockinette stitch over 4" (10cm)
0 LACE	10-count crochet thread (fingering)	000–1 (1.5–2.25mm)	33–40 sts
1 SUPER FINE	Sock, baby (fingering)	1–2 (2.25–3.25mm)	27–32 sts
2 FINE	Lightweight DK, baby (sport)	3–5 (3.25–3.75mm)	23–26 sts
3 LIGHT	DK (light worsted)	5–7 (3.75–4.5mm)	21–24 sts
4 MEDIUM	Aran (worsted, afghan)	7–9 (4.5–5.5mm)	16–20 sts
5 BULKY	Chunky (craft, rug)	9–11 (5.5–8mm)	12–15 sts
6 SUPER BULKY	Bulky, roving	11 and larger (8mm and larger)	6–11 sts

ACKNOWLEDGMENTS

A huge thank you to the following people who have all helped to make this book happen:

As always, thank you to Rowan for their wonderful yarns and to Kate Buller for allowing me to use these yarns to bring the teddies to life! To Sharon Brant whose support and invaluable advice I'd be lost without. To the team at Collins & Brown and in particular Miriam Hyslop for her help and guidance. To Sarah and Margaret for their kind words and help with the knitting. Lastly, a big thank you to Jez whose love and support as always was unwavering.

PICTURE CREDITS

Photography by Rachel Whiting
Front cover photography by Mark Winwood
Illustrations by Kang Chen